Maurice Segran

The Cure´s niece

Maurice Segran

The Cure's niece

ISBN/EAN: 9783741192777

Manufactured in Europe, USA, Canada, Australia, Japa

Cover: Foto ©Andreas Hilbeck / pixelio.de

Manufactured and distributed by brebook publishing software (www.brebook.com)

Maurice Segran

The Cure´s niece

THE CURÉ'S NIECE.

LONDON:
ROBSON AND SONS, PRINTERS, PANCRAS ROAD, N.W.

THE
CURÉ'S NIECE.

BY

MAURICE SEGRAN.

LONDON: BURNS AND OATES.
1879.

THE CURÉ'S NIECE.

FIRST PART.

CHAPTER I.

WHY, I should like to ask, is there such a pool of water opposite the front door of the presbytery? I am well aware, of course, that there are many things, as well as people, which are not in their proper place in this world. But this deep pool, the water of which is so cold, was certainly especially ill placed.

Moreover, how is it possible it could have been formed? It is true that a great deal of rain had fallen the preceding evening; but it is also true that the night before, the Curé, who liked to have everything neat and orderly about him, had had the soil carefully levelled and beaten in front of his poor little home. He had also very judiciously ordered two channels to be dug, so that in case of a heavy pourdown the surplus water might be carried to the ditch below. He had employed in this hydraulic operation a big long-legged fellow called Joseph, who was always studiously occupied in doing nothing, and who spent his life in going about the village, or wandering through the fields, with his arms swinging to and fro, sniffing the breeze, and whistling all kinds of odd tunes. In order to induce him, by way of an extraordinary exception, to take the work in hand, you may most likely imagine that the Curé had been obliged to promise him good wages. If, however, he had done so, it would have been tantamount to saying to him, 'Go and get tipsy.' Instead of that he told him that he would make him a present of a pair of new trousers; those which Joseph had been wearing for a long time past being full of holes and rents, which greatly annoyed the honest fellow. For although Joseph was not influenced by considerations of modesty, he was sensible to certain currents of air, which became day by day more and more disagreeable to him; for autumn was approaching, and the wind was becoming very keen. These new trousers were therefore a great temptation to him, and he had consented to do the work; but only, it is needless to say, in the character of an amateur. As, however, he was very closely watched during the performance of his task, he ended by carrying it through very creditably.

I repeat, therefore, that the pool was incomprehensible. It would have been still more extraordinary if the good Curé, on returning home rather late from the château, entirely preoccupied with some very serious subjects for thought, which the old Marquise had imparted to him, had entered his house without putting his foot into the puddle. He did not fail to do so; and as he was one of those determined kind of men who never do anything by halves, his left foot immediately followed his right; consequently M. le Curé crossed the threshold of the presbytery with a pint of water in each shoe.

It was on that account that, instead of entering into the little parlour on the right-hand side of the passage, where his niece was awaiting him rather anxiously, and reading by the light of a tallow-candle the eighteenth chapter of the first book of the *Imitation*, he turned to the left, and in a couple of strides stepped upon the flags of the kitchen-floor, where the water ran out of his shoes without doing a great deal of damage. Not that in the parlour on the right hand there was either a carpet or white boards to be careful about; on the contrary, the floor was composed of nothing more luxurious than a pavement of tiles; but old Johanna had only quite lately rubbed and polished them, and so it would have been a thousand pities to spoil them.

'Jesus! have you been in the pond, M. le Curé?'

asked Johanna, who, seated near a small stove, was pretending to knit a stocking, over which the fatigue she had undergone during the day made her fall asleep every evening between the eleventh and twelfth stitches.

Stupefied, and with her eyes only half open, she looked at her master through her spectacles.

The Curé did not answer. He took off his *tricorne*, wiped his forehead, looked with indifference at the pool of water which was forming round him, then slightly shrugging one shoulder,

'Bah!' he said, in a good-humoured tone, 'it is only a little water.'

'Only a little!' exclaimed Johanna, rising from her seat.

A young girl appeared at the door through which the Curé had just entered.

'Uncle, what is the matter? Why have you returned so late? Why were you sent for in such a hurry to the château? Has any misfortune happened?'

The voice was sweet and gentle, but the questions were asked a little hastily. The Curé raised his finger in a grave but not very severe manner.

'Four questions all at once, Mariette; it is a great number. One only is often one too many.'

'I was uneasy, uncle,' said Mariette.

'And not in the least curious?' asked the Curé.

'But his shoes are full of water, and he will have one of his attacks of rheumatism,' cried out Johanna.

In a moment, and without being asked whether he liked it or not, the Curé was obliged to sit down on a wooden chair close beside the stove, in which there were still some remains of a fire, and made to take off his shoes.

'His best pair!' murmured Johanna to herself, putting them near the fire to dry, and she shook her head on seeing that this best pair had already begun to wear out.

Her master laughed gently. It was a good face which the priest had. A large aquiline nose, bearing testimony to the energy of his character; a thoughtful brow; eyes that were at once keen and benevolent; a firm well-shaped mouth; and hair tinged with gray.

It was a little surprising to see that a resemblance existed between so characteristic and masculine a face and that of Mariette, delicate and refined as hers was. Blue eyes, dreamily reposing beneath eyebrows which were rather black than brown; a sweet and pensive mouth, which rarely broke out into a smile; a smooth and polished brow, across which eighteen years had scarcely passed; and a charming pink-and-white complexion, relieved by dark-brown hair arranged in close plaits, which failed, however, to disguise its abundance. In the whole appearance a nameless something, an air of aristocratic refinement, which seemed a little incongruous when compared with the poverty of Mariette's costume, consisting of a cotton dress, which was made in a scrupulously simple fashion, and that was all.

If the niece were poor in regard to dresses, the uncle was not rich in respect to *soutanes*, for the one he wore was patched all over; and yet he also, spite of a weather-beaten and tanned complexion—spite, moreover, of sunburnt hands—showed indescribable signs of good birth.

Johanna, who was still continuing to prognosticate gout and rheumatism, had meanwhile gone to get a pair of dry stockings for her master, and, by way of slippers, a pair of old shoes. The two women having retired, the Curé slowly changed his shoes, not without grumbling, and yet smiling at being forced to indulge in so great a luxury of precautions; then he called for his niece. She came back, carrying her *Imitation* in one hand and her candle in the other.

'Put it out,' said her uncle; 'Johanna's candle is sufficient. Now let us finish our evening in the kitchen, and sit down near the remains of the fire.'

Taking a chair, and crossing her two little hands —a trifle reddened by familiarity with the sun—upon her knees, Mariette said to the Curé,

'At the risk of being again suspected of curiosity, uncle, I cannot help renewing my question as to what has happened at the château?'

'All that has happened, Mariette, is that Madame la Marquise wanted to speak to me.'

'She is not ill, is she?'

'No—that is to say, yes.'

'No—that is to say, yes! What does that mean, uncle?'

'That means, little one, that Madame la Marquise suddenly fell ill, but that she is better now.'

'As she sent for you in such haste, uncle, it was doubtless because she was seriously ill?'

The Curé appeared to be plunged in thought, and made no answer.

'I see,' said Mariette, softly smiling; 'I am evidently too curious.'

'You curious!' exclaimed her uncle, looking at her with an affectionate expression in his eyes. 'I was only joking when I said so, dear little one. I know perfectly well that if you question me; it is because you are anxious about your old friend. Do not be uneasy. She is not in any danger. Yet it is possible I may be sent for again to-night. If you hear any one knock, do not be alarmed, and do not get up. Johanna must not get up either. I will go down and open the door myself.'

'You will not go out—at least not alone, uncle! The servant who comes from the château will wait for you, will not he? and will he not also accompany you on your return?'

The Curé, evidently occupied with his own thoughts, did not hear Mariette, nor did she venture to address any further questions to him, and the evening thus passed more silently than usual. At nine o'clock the Curé recited night prayers, and the household retired to rest.

Mariette was greatly astonished, a little while afterwards, to hear her uncle walking, for a long time, up and down his little room, as though he had not been able to find the sleep which, in general, never allowed itself to await his summons.

In the middle of the night there occurred an additional cause for surprise. The prediction made by the Curé was realised, and some one knocked at the door of the presbytery. Suddenly aroused by the noise, the young girl awoke, heard her uncle go down stairs, unfasten the lock of the door, and soon afterwards set out with the person who had come to fetch him, and who was a servant belonging to the château. What could have happened? Serious, indeed, must be the reasons which had caused the Curé to be sent for at such an hour. Mariette indulged in a hundred conjectures; at the hundred and first she fell asleep.

Later on, during the night, something fresh took place! Another knock was heard at the door. Could it be the Curé, who had come back, and who had forgotten to take his keys? In a moment Mariette, putting on her dress, ran to the window.

'I will come down and open the door, uncle. Johanna is doubtless so fast asleep that she does not hear you.'

But a voice she did not recognise replied in a half whisper,

'M. le Curé wishes you to go to the château, mademoiselle. I am come for you.'

'My uncle is not ill, is he?' said Mariette, in a frightened tone.

'No, mademoiselle. It is for Madame la Marquise, I think.'

It was Lambert, the old valet, who thus spoke.

'I am coming down,' said Mariette; and she hastily finished dressing herself.

On leaving her room, she came in contact with Johanna, who, at last roused and bewildered, had hastened to see what was happening. Mariette, hurried though she was, felt obliged to tell her what was the matter, and even to repeat her words, for Johanna could not comprehend what it all meant, and asked one question after another.

'Jesus!' she exclaimed, when at last she knew all; 'is Madame la Marquise actually dying? And M. le Curé is gone out in his old shoes without heels! He will have cold feet; he will be ill—I am certain of it! His other shoes will, perhaps, be dry by this time. Wait a moment, mademoiselle; I will go and see.'

Then, calling out at the bottom of the stairs, she added:

'Here they are, mademoiselle; they are quite dry; I had put them in the oven. Give them to him as soon as you reach the château.'

Mariette took the shoes in her hand, and left the house. She would have liked to run, or, at any rate, to walk very fast; but Lambert was not able to keep up with her. Regulating her impatient steps by the slower ones of the old servant, she began to question him. It was in vain. He either knew nothing or would say nothing, excepting that his mistress was ill; that M. le Curé was with her, and that he had desired his niece should be sent for.

Was Madame la Marquise seriously ill?

Lambert could not say.

Had the doctor been sent for?

Lambert did not know.

Mariette could gain no information. At last they had left the village behind them. The château rose in front, a sombre mass, in which lights shone forth here and there from some of the windows. They crossed the courts, passed under the porch, and found themselves in an immense vestibule.

'Come into this room, Mademoiselle Mariette,' said Lambert, as he introduced the young girl into a vast and solemn-looking drawing-room, dimly lighted by a wax-taper placed upon the marble chimneypiece.

'I will go up-stairs and inform M. le Curé of your arrival; he will then tell me whether he wishes you to join him.'

Lambert accordingly disappeared and closed the door, whilst Mariette seated herself upon the chair that was nearest to it, and began mechanically to gaze at the scantily-lighted room, which she had never seen before, because when she had hitherto visited the château she had always been taken into the private apartments of the Marquise. Her attention was suddenly attracted by a sonorous yawn, which came from a dark corner. There, upon a sofa of antique form, a man was extended. Stretching himself, he sat up, and yawned again, closing his eyes, as though he would have very much liked to resume the sleep which had doubtless been broken by the opening and shutting of the door.

Mariette rose, and in her bewilderment was about to take flight when the sleeper perceived her. He left his sofa and approached her, in order that he might endeavour to find out who she was.

'Mademoiselle Mariette, I believe?' he said, in a tone of surprise, tempered by politeness. 'Really, mademoiselle, I did not at all expect—I was fast asleep.'

'Pardon, M. le Marquis,' said Mariette, in a slightly agitated tone; 'I did not see you. It was Lambert who brought me in here. He was, of course, unaware that you were in the room. I came to the château because I was sent for by my uncle, who is at present with Madame la Marquise, and I am waiting—But I will go into the vestibule.'

And Mariette went towards the door. But the Marquis, recalling her, courteously begged her to sit down in a large easy-chair, which he rolled towards her. The young girl thanked him, and again expressed a wish to retire. In her confusion she allowed one of her uncle's shoes, which she was holding in her hand, hidden under her shawl, to fall on the ground. The shoe made a great noise as it rolled along the floor.

'You are losing something, mademoiselle.'

'It is nothing,' Mariette hastily replied.

And she bent down to pick up the shoe, but whilst doing so she let the other fall. Then she hastily stretched out her hands and endeavoured to find them in the half light which prevailed in the room; but she sought in vain.

'Allow me to help you,' said the Marquis; and so saying he went towards the mantelpiece for the candle.

Coming back to the young girl he stumbled over one of the shoes, stooped and picked it up.

'Why,' he exclaimed, in an astonished tone, 'it is a shoe!'

And at that moment Mariette found the other.

'Yes,' she murmured. 'Excuse me, it is mine—it is my uncle's—it was Johanna—'

And she became so bewildered that she could not say another word. The Marquis, who was holding his candlestick in one hand and the shoe in his other, looked at the young girl, and appeared to be making an effort to preserve his gravity. The light of the candle shone upon his face, and showed him to be a young man of hardly twenty-five years of age, of expressive features and an elegant figure. All at once he burst into a fit of laughter.

'A thousand pardons, mademoiselle,' he said; 'but we have really such a droll appearance, looking at each other in this way, and each of us holding a shoe. Permit me to relieve you of yours.'

Mariette would have been very glad to retain possession of it; but the young man smilingly took it out of her hand, and put it beside the other upon an elegant lackered table, on which he also placed the candlestick. Then he made Mariette sit down, whilst he seated himself beside her. The young girl immediately began to explain as briefly as possible that the shoes were intended for her uncle, who had set off in such haste, when summoned by Madame la Marquise, that he had not even had time to put on a proper pair.

'I am not surprised,' the young Marquis kindly aid. 'M. le Curé is accustomed to forget himself for the sake of others, and no selfish considerations restrain him whenever there is a question of rendering a kindness to any one. He has already been a long time with my grandmother.'

'Is she very ill?' Mariette timidly inquired.

'No, I do not think so,' the young man carelessly answered. 'She is a little—a little agitated; that is all.'

And he sank back in his easy-chair, whilst endeavouring to repress a slight yawn.

'It was M. le Curé who sent for you, was it not, mademoiselle?' he pursued. 'That was what you told me a minute ago, did you not? Might I inquire why he wished you to come here?'

'I have not the least idea, M. le Marquis; but it seems to me that Lambert is a long time in coming back. Is it possible that he has not seen my uncle?'

'Do not be afraid, mademoiselle; Lambert is a model of exactness. If you are obliged to wait, it is most probably because my grandmother has again become a little—excited, and that she wishes the good Curé to remain beside her. But I at any rate have no cause to complain of the delay, since it procures me the prolonged enjoyment of your society, which gives me far more pleasure than sleeping upon this terribly hard old sofa. To tell you the truth, I do not know why I am here, excepting that M. le Curé begged me to wait in the drawing-room. I have done so, though

I cannot imagine of what use I can be. So here we are, both of us; and neither the one nor the other knows what we are wanted for. Really it is too amusing.'

And the Marquis once more began to laugh. Mariette felt, however, as though his gaiety were a little out of place, and she hardly knew how to answer him. Just at that moment the sound of footsteps was heard approaching, the door opened, and the Curé made his appearance.

CHAPTER II.

'Ah, here you are little one!' the Curé hastily exclaimed. 'Come, I am going to take you to Madame la Marquise. Pardon, M. le Marquis, I did not see you. Your grandmother is very ill.'

'I am exceedingly grieved to hear it, M. le Curé; but she will soon be better. Your exhortations will quickly restore her to composure.'

'I am, on the contrary, afraid that I shall not be able to afford her any relief.'

'You are wrong to say so, M. le Curé. You can do much under present circumstances.'

'Permit me, M. le Marquis,' said the Curé, in a very serious tone, 'to apply the words you have just spoken to yourself. It is *you* who are wrong to use such expressions as you have just done. You are perfectly well aware that I am powerless in this matter. If there be any one who can do *all* that is required, any one who by a word can restore peace of mind to our dear and excellent suffering friend, is it not you, M. le Marquis?'

These words were accompanied by a very significant look directed towards the young man. He bore it with indifference, and remained quietly stretched in his easy-chair.

'There are trials which kill one, M. le Marquis,' said the Curé, with animation; 'think of the responsibility—'

'Pardon me, M. le Curé,' broke in the Marquis, with an air of calmness and perfect self-composure; 'here are a pair of shoes which Mademoiselle Mariette has brought for you, and which she has forgotten, I think, to give you.'

Then, in the most amiable manner possible, he pointed with his finger to the unfortunate pair of shoes lying upon the round table.

The Curé made an involuntary movement, as though he had felt the impertinence; but he replied, with a great deal of calmness,

'Thank you, M. le Marquis. Thank you also, Mariette, for having thought of me. Only it would have been better not to have brought such rustic shoes into a drawing-room, and above all not to have placed them on a table.'

'It is I who committed that solecism,' remarked the young man; 'and Mademoiselle Mariette—'

'I must not prolong our conversation,' the Curé in his turn broke in. 'My patient is expecting me. Your grandmother has desired me to tell you that a little repose is absolutely necessary for her, and that

C

she desires to avoid, just at present, any fresh explanations.'

'Very well, M. le Curé; but I suppose you will not object to my going myself to inquire how my grandmother is?'

'Madame la Marquise has desired Lambert not to allow any one to enter her room.'

'Excepting yourself doubtless, M. le Curé?'

'Yes, excepting myself, M. le Marquis.'

'And excepting, perhaps, mademoiselle, your niece.'

'Yes, excepting also my niece.'

'Just so: everything is as it should be. I must wait, then, until to-morrow to see whether it will be well that I should prolong my sojourn here. Meanwhile, I suppose there is nothing to prevent me from retiring to my room?'

'Nothing, M. le Marquis. I asked you a little while ago to await me here, because I had hoped that perhaps a favourable opportunity would present itself; but nothing of the kind has taken place.'

The Marquis rose carelessly and pulled the bell. A valet in handsome livery obeyed the summons.

'I am going to my room, Tipp,' said the young man shortly; 'light me.'

The valet, in a most unceremonious manner, at once took the candlestick which was standing on the table.

'Well, fool, are you going to leave M. le Curé in the dark?' exclaimed the Marquis. 'Go and light the other candle.'

Then, bowing with a graceful air to the Curé and his niece, the young Marquis, preceded by his valet, who walked backwards, candlestick in hand, went out of the drawing-room, the door of which he neglected to shut.

The Curé, after having closed it, turned pensively to his niece. After a long silence, which Mariette did not venture to break,

'My child,' he said to her, 'many sad things are taking place here. The less you hear about them the less you will understand them; and it is better that it should be so. Nevertheless, I am about to take you to the aged Marquise. She is ill. She requires care and attention such as I dare not allow her to receive from the servants who are at the château, because sometimes, in the height of her fever, she says things which it would not be right they should hear. You must watch over her; you must not leave her for a moment. Follow me.'

They accordingly ascended in silence the wide steps of the oaken staircase, which, creaking as they proceeded on their way, awoke distant echoes in the deserted corridors. After having traversed several dimly-lighted and spacious apartments, covered by thick carpets which stifled the sound of their footsteps, they reached a door, beside which the aged Lambert was seated.

'Madame la Marquise has not asked for me?' inquired the Curé, in a low voice.

Lambert made a sign in the negative, and without pronouncing a word gently pushed open one of the folding-doors, which was not quite closed. The Curé desired his niece to precede him, and following her, he closed the door behind them. They then found themselves in a boudoir, illuminated only by the light which came from an adjoining room, through a wide doorway hung with drapery. Mariette paused on the threshold of this inner chamber. At the farther end was an immense bed, overhung by a canopy supported on heavy pillars. In the middle of the room, near a table covered with a dark velvet cover, and on which were two large candelabra, a lady was seated in an easy-chair. Her gray hair, which had escaped from her headdress, fell in disorder upon her shoulders, and encircled a haggard wrinkled face as white as wax, denoting extreme old age, but also discovering the remains of great beauty. This weird-looking face was illuminated, as it were, by a pair of large eyes, which were still full of fire. Her two hands were placed upon the arms of her chair; hands astonishingly small, yellow as ivory, and ornamented with rings which were half concealed by the wrinkles of the skin. The lady was gazing fixedly before her;

the expression of her eyes was both proud, ardent, and vague; one of her feet, from which a silken slipper had fallen, feverishly tapped the carpet.

'Madame la Marquise,' said the Curé, advancing, 'here is my niece, who, I trust, will find in you a docile patient.'

The Marquise started and rose from her seat with a vivacity which was hardly to be expected from a person of her age; then, drawing herself up to the full height of her majestic figure, she addressed the Curé very severely, and as though she had not understood the meaning of the words which he had just addressed to her.

'Well,' she exclaimed, 'have you seen that unnatural boy? What is he doing? What does he say? Does he continue obstinate? Yes, of course he does. Has he asked you how many days, how many hours, I may still have to live? Does he not think that Death is obliging us to wait a long time for him?'

The Curé made no answer. The Marquise walked up and down the room for a moment with feeble steps; then, all at once, directing towards the Curé a harsh look, which perfectly harmonised with the haughty expression of her physiognomy,

'You do not answer me,' she said. 'You dare not; you are afraid of causing blushes of shame to mount to my withered brow by telling me into what an abyss of abasement the last of the Marquis de Saissières has fallen!'

'Compose yourself, madame, compose yourself; and, above all, be resigned,' said the Curé, with a mixture of firmness and gentleness.

The Marquise drew near to the table.

'You are aware,' said she, leaning her trembling hands upon it, ' that I have had my share of trials. I have submitted to them courageously. I have seen my son and my husband die, and I have not died myself. But to behold my last remaining hope in this world cast down; to feel myself humiliated in the person of the last scion of the old race—if *that* is not enough, it is at any rate very much. One can endure everything except shame.'

She had mechanically taken up from the table a mother-of-pearl paper-knife. Whilst pronouncing these last words she snapped it in two; then, as though the effort, feeble though it was, had exhausted her strength, she tottered and stretched out her arms in search of support. Mariette went quickly up to her, held her in her arms, and then made her sit down upon her chair, addressing to her meanwhile, in a whisper, some affectionate expressions. The agitated features of the Marquise gradually regained composure, and fixing her eyes, a few moments ago so sombre in expression, but now full of benevolence, upon the young girl,

I am glad to see you, dear one,' she said gently.

'You have done well to come to me. Do not leave me; I feel as though your presence did me good. How is it you were able to come at such an hour as this, poor child? It must be very late. I had already gone to bed, but I could not sleep, and I got up again. Then I became confused and agitated; for you see, dear child, I am in great trouble—very great trouble; and I sent for your uncle. What has become of him? Ah, there he is, my kind good friend. Come, sit down, both of you, close to me.'

'No, Madame la Marquise,' said the Curé. 'I must leave you now; but I will come back and see you to-morrow—or rather to-day, for morning is about to dawn. I leave you in Mariette's hands. She will help you to get into bed again. Promise me to try and sleep a little; you are in great need of repose.'

As he left the room he said in a whisper to Mariette, 'Do not leave her; Lambert will remain within call to summon her maids should you require them, and he will not allow any one to disturb you. I will go and remind him once more of the duty he has to perform.'

As soon as she found herself alone with her patient, Mariette persuaded her to return to bed, and soon afterwards she saw her fall asleep. Feeling very drowsy herself, she lay back in an easy-chair. When she again opened her eyes, day had dawned, but the Marquise still slept. Her slumber was, however, troubled and feverish, and from time to time she uttered some incoherent words, until all at once she opened her eyes and sat up in bed, looking at Mariette with surprise and anger.

'What are you doing here?' she abruptly asked.

'Do you not remember me, madame?' inquired the frightened girl.

'Yes, certainly, little one,' answered Madame de Saissières, taking her by the hand; 'but when I first awoke out of a frightful dream I fancied that I saw, sitting there, that wretched—Pardon me, child; sometimes my poor old head gets confused. Assist me to rise, or rather ring the bell for my maids.'

Mariette, however, begged, and the Marquise gave her permission, to help her to rise. The aged lady had some difficulty in getting out of bed, and seemed exhausted by the effort. As soon as she was wrapped in an ample dressing-gown of white cashmere, and stretched upon a sofa, she again desired Mariette to ring the bell; and when the young girl objected, the Marquise, knitting her brow, reiterated her request, or rather her commands, in so absolute a tone, that Mariette did not venture any longer to oppose her.

Two maids entered the room. The Marquise received their services, and then had her sofa rolled into the boudoir, requesting Mariette to follow her, and desiring that breakfast should be served.

'I must not allow you to die of hunger in my own house, my child,' she said, with a feeble smile. 'In this apartment, at any rate, I am at home.'

She gazed with melancholy pleasure at pretty little Mariette eating her breakfast with a good appetite, but she would not herself partake of any refreshment. When the repast was ended, remarking that Mariette was looking with an air of interest at the pictures with which the boudoir was decorated,

'You think them all very beautiful,' she said.

'Certainly, madame,' answered Mariette, with some hesitation; 'but my reason for looking at them is because they recall to me the pictures which, as a child, I used to admire in my father's house.'

'That is natural, my dear. But when I see you in such a simple costume, I always forget that you were born in another rank of life. Yet do you know, when I think of the luxury by which I am surrounded, when I recall to mind my arrival here in state fifty years ago, and when I look at myself, such as I am now, I long that I had strength to destroy everything around me which awakes a remembrance of the past. I am stifled; open the door, if you please.'

Mariette opened a large glass door which gave access to a balcony, whence there was a view of the park, with its extensive lawns and its majestic trees.

'The fresh air does me good,' said the Marquise, uncovering her bosom, heedless of the remonstrances addressed to her by Mariette, who was afraid lest she should suffer from the keen morning air. 'Let me breathe,' she exclaimed.

All at once she seized the young girl's arm, and with her other hand pointing to a distant part of the park.

'There, there!' she cried out, in a trembling voice. 'Do you see her? Do you see them both? Look, look! They are just about to disappear at the turning of the road.'

Mariette glanced towards the park, and thought that she really saw some one in a distant avenue; but the apparition only lasted a moment. When she turned her eyes towards the Marquise she was frightened to see her looking deadly pale, and her eyes closed. Just then the Curé entered. At the sound of his footsteps the Marquise opened her eyes. Bending towards the priest, and stretching out one hand in the direction of the window, she exclaimed,

'I have seen them!'

The Curé, without answering, made a sign to his niece, and opening a door concealed by tapestry, which led to a long gallery hung with portraits,

'Walk up and down there until I call you,' he said. 'I wish to be alone with the Marquise.'

Mariette paced the gallery for a long time. Suddenly the sound of the Marquise's voice reached the young girl's ears, and warned her that she ran the risk of involuntarily surprising the secrets of a confidential interview. She therefore retired to the other end of the corridor, and seated herself upon a bench. More than an hour had passed away when she saw a door softly open at the opposite extremity of the gallery. The young Marquis de Saissières appeared at it, and without perceiving Mariette, trod with cautious steps towards the door which opened into the apartment of Madame de Saissières. Just as he was about to open it he paused, as though struck by the sound of voices, listened for a moment, and then turned back with an impatient gesture. At that moment he perceived the Curé's niece. Starting, he advanced rapidly towards her.

'What are you doing here, young girl?' he abruptly asked, and with a glance which recalled the expression she had noticed the evening before in the eyes of the Marquise. Hurt by so uncourteous a mode of address, she replied,

'I am waiting here until Madame la Marquise de Saissières wishes me to return to her, and I am staying at the château by her express wish.'

'It is the Curé who is with her just now, is it not?' asked the young man, in the same imperious tone.

After a moment's hesitation Mariette replied, with much gentleness and composure,

'Your servants will be able to inform you, Monsieur le Marquis.'

'But it is you to whom I have addressed the question,' he said, with irritation.

Mariette rose without making any reply. The Marquis turned away, and quickly regained the door by which he had entered. As he was about to cross the threshold he paused, and after standing still, and, as it seemed, reflecting, for a moment, he retraced his steps.

'*Mon Dieu*, mademoiselle, I am very absurd,' he said, in a tone which was perfectly courteous, but slightly agitated. 'I really do not know what I have been saying to you. My grandmother's valet having refused to allow me to enter her room, I was attempting to gain access to it by another door; for it is absolutely necessary that I should speak to her. Finding that she was not alone, I felt somewhat irritated. I hope you will excuse me.'

Then, after having made some inquiries respecting his grandmother's health, he bowed and withdrew. A few moments afterwards the Curé came out of Madame de Saissières' apartment, and said to his niece,

'You are going to remain at the château, my child, for a few days. No objection, if you please. It costs me a great deal to be obliged to part with you, but it is necessary. You may be useful to Madame la Marquise; I may even say that you are necessary to her. The prospect of having you beside her has already restored her to composure and given her consolation. I will come here every day; and, moreover, if anything were to happen you could send for me at once.'

Mariette thought it was right she should inform her uncle of the apparition of the young Marquis. The Curé listened in silence, then he said,

'It is well. Precautions must be taken which will prevent Madame de Saissières from being exposed to importunities which would be her death. Do not be afraid that any further attempt of the kind will be made.'

Mariette was installed that same day in a small room adjacent to the one occupied by the Marquise. The young girl felt her heart swell on finding herself thus a prisoner, so to say, in such a sombre dwelling; but accustomed, as she was, to forget herself and think only of her duty, no matter how modest and humble it might be, she did not allow any sign of her feelings to appear; on the contrary, she endeavoured to maintain towards her old friend the gentle and tranquil mien which was habitual to her. She was speedily repaid for the effort she made by seeing that Madame de Saissières was rendered happy in her society, and that she was regaining, little by little, composure and self-control.

CHAPTER III.

Two days passed very quietly. The Curé came several times to see the Marquise, and had some long conversations with her, during which Mariette was able to ramble wherever she liked, in the picture-gallery or in the park. She never met the young Marquis; and as no one now mentioned his name, she took it for granted that he had left the château.

The evening of the third day the Marquise, rousing herself from a long meditation, which Mariette had respected, and during which she had yielded herself up to her own thoughts, said all at once,

'My child, to-morrow I must receive my lawyer, and speak to him respecting a very important decision at which I have just arrived, thanks to your uncle, who has helped me in this my hour of trial. But there still remain, I must confess, some doubts in my mind. The circumstances in which I am placed are very serious. If my son were still alive, he would decide for me, because it is the future of his child which is in the balance. Would he have approved of the decision I have come to? I anxiously ask myself. Why cannot he let me know his wishes? Why should there be such a complete separation between the dead and those who lament them? Is it not frightful to think that the son whom I so dearly loved, and to whom I shall so soon be reunited, sees me and hears me at this all-important moment, that he will perhaps disapprove of what I am about to do, and yet that he is not permitted to warn me by a word or a sign, no matter how mysterious it might be? You are about to accompany me into the room where he died, and where I have gone so often, since that terrible day, to weep and to meditate. I shall, perhaps, there receive some inspiration. I will read once more the journal, to which during his illness—his long agony, I ought rather to say—he consigned, at my request, his daily thoughts and reflections.'

Mariette entreated the Marquise to spare herself a renewal of such cruel emotions; but the aged lady persisted, and she was obliged to obey.

The two women first traversed the picture-gallery, and then a long vaulted corridor. The vacillating light cast by the candle which Mariette carried caused their magnified shadows to dance behind them. Leaning upon the arm of her young companion, the Marquise advanced with difficulty, and the sound of her sighs mingled with the rustling of the long-trained antique silk dress which she wore.

'It was here,' she said, pausing before a deeply recessed door, 'it was through this private entrance that I always passed into the room occupied by my son.'

Just as she was about to enter she halted, and bowing her head, said, in a half whisper,

'It is a long time since I ventured hither. Hence it is, doubtless, that my emotion is so great. What a remembrance, dear child, such a deathbed is! To see death approach, little by little, slowly but implacably, in order to snatch away from you the being whom you love! And not to be able to do anything except pray, pray, pray, and always, alas, in vain! During the last days of his life he suffered so much that I summoned courage to entreat God to abridge his tortures. It was a petition which was as vain as those which had preceded it. For death would not come. It was a horrible and interminable agony! I can still hear the death-rattle! O, who can ever conceive what I suffered, kneeling at the foot of his bed!'

Madame de Saissières was seized with so violent a trembling that Mariette could hardly support her.

'In the name of Heaven, madame,' exclaimed the Curé's niece, 'return to your own room! Your strength will fail you if you enter that chamber.'

'I blush at my weakness,' said the Marquise, in a broken voice; 'nevertheless, I will go in. If I have not strength to remain there, I will at least take away the journal written by my son.'

'You shall do nothing of the kind, madame,' cried the young girl firmly. 'I was wrong to have allowed you to come hither. Return to your apartments. If you wish to have the manuscript of which you speak, I will come back and fetch it.'

Uttering these words with a firmness of which no one would have believed her capable, Mariette put her arm round the waist of the Marquise and led her away. When she had brought her back to her chamber, and saw that she had regained composure, she offered to go and get the journal of the deceased Marquis. Madame de Saissières gratefully accepted her proposal, and gave into her hand the key of a bureau, which she told her was in the room, and where the manuscript was placed.

Taking her taper once more in her hand, Mariette returned alone to the mortuary chamber. As she entered it, she shivered involuntarily; and although quite free from all superstitious weakness, it was not without feeling her heart beat faster than usual that she cast her eyes about her. The room was of great size, the walls covered with sombre hangings, and the furniture with leather that was almost black. Upon the table lay a few books, whilst some papers which were scattered about gave the room the appearance of being still occupied. In an alcove draped with heavy velvet curtains, Mariette perceived a bed; and beside it a large bureau with a cylindrical top, in which

D

the manuscript was kept After having dwelt for a
moment upon the sorrowful tragedy of which the
chamber had been the scene, the young girl tried to
open the bureau; but the lock resisted her efforts.
Having one of her hands occupied with holding the
candlestick, she put it down upon the table which
stood in the centre of the room. At that moment she
distinctly heard a creaking sound proceed from the
further end of the alcove, and turned round trembling;
but she saw nothing. Standing still, she listened, and
heard nothing excepting the agitated beating of her
heart. If she had followed her first impulse, she
would have quitted the room at once. Annoyed at
being a prey to the puerile fears which she had so
frequently heard her uncle condemn, she determined
to make an effort to enter the alcove, and to cast a
glance around it. She accordingly did so; but at the
very moment when, with outstretched arm, she was
passing her candlestick between the curtains, the
taper was suddenly extinguished in an inexplicable
manner. Frightened by the darkness, Mariette was
just about to scream. She was, however, able to restrain herself; and, suppressing her agitation, endeavoured to find her way back to the door whereby she
had entered; but without success. After having first
come in contact with the table, and then with an easy-chair, and after that with other pieces of furniture, she
paused; and, overcome by agitation, was half-resolved

to summon some one to her aid. She determined, nevertheless, to make a last attempt. After having endeavoured to recall to mind, as well as she could, the part of the room in which she stood, she began to walk slowly, with her hands stretched out in front of her. She fancied she was approaching the door, when, on the contrary, she found herself entering the alcove. Shivering, spite of her courage, she lowered her hands in order to assure herself that the bed was really there, and found that, in fact, it was; but her hand came in contact with another hand lying there, and which, though she had only touched it very lightly, seemed to her to be strangely cold.

It was too much for the nerves of the poor child. She uttered a stifled cry, and fainted.

CHAPTER IV.

WHEN she came to herself, after a lapse of time the duration of which it was impossible for her to calculate, Mariette found that she was stretched upon a settee in the picture-gallery. She was alone; beside her was her taper, relighted and placed upon a pier-table. As she moved, something escaped from her hand and fell on the ground. It was the key of the bureau, which she had in vain endeavoured to open in the chamber of the deceased Marquis. And yet she fancied she had left the key in the lock—indeed, she was sure of it; for she remembered everything that had taken place clearly and accurately. But it was not that, after all, which most surprised her. How had she been able to get back to the picture-gallery? What was it she had heard in that awful room? And what had she touched upon the bed? She could not help asking herself whether she were not out of her mind. Always on her guard, however, against being carried away by her imagination, and feeling herself incapable at that moment of calmly reflecting on what had occurred, and of arriving at any reasonable explanation of it, she endeavoured only to think of what there remained for her to do, clearly seeing that the Marquise was the last person in the world to whom she could speak of so strange an adventure. But how long was it since she had left the aged lady? Would she not be already feeling astonished at her prolonged absence? What answer could she make to her questions? In any case she must return to her as quickly as possible. Still trembling, but already mistress of herself, Mariette regained the apartments of the Marquise.

'What has become of you, little one?' she exclaimed, with vivacity. 'Where have you been staying so long? I was just about to come and fetch you.'

Mariette briefly answered that she had not been able to open the drawer of the bureau to which the Marquise had directed her, and that, her candle having gone out, she had become a little frightened when she found herself in the dark.

'Poor darling,' said Madame de Saissières, 'your voice still trembles, and you are quite pale. I am sure you must have been terribly alarmed. Why did you not tell me that you did not like to go back alone? Do not let us think anything more about the manuscript. I will go and get it myself to-morrow morning.'

And she lavished the most tender caresses upon the young girl.

Mariette did not fail the next day to relate her adventure to her uncle as soon as she saw him. Incredulous at first, he made her repeat the story again. After reflecting for a moment he seemed about to say something, but on second thoughts merely murmured to himself,

'It was he, doubtless. Happily it is all coming to an end. They will soon leave, I trust. The Marquise has chosen the wisest course, I believe. I have earnestly prayed that God would enlighten her.'

And Mariette was not allowed to know anything more.

On that day strangers came to the château. No doubt they were the lawyers of whom the Marquise had spoken the evening before. They held long conferences with her, and the young girl was left meanwhile alone. She spent the time in walking about that portion of the park which had been assigned to her as a place where she might take exercise, and which had been reserved for the private use of the Marquise. These solitary hours were productive of good to her, and helped her to recover from the agitation she had undergone the previous evening, though she could not help dwelling upon what had taken place, and would have liked to return to the chamber. Not having asked permission from her uncle, however, she felt as if she dare not, and therefore resolved to speak to him about it the following day.

When, towards evening, she was summoned to go to the Marquise she found her much calmer than she had expected. Nevertheless the old lady's face bore traces of abundant tears.

'Come and sit down near me, my child,' she said, with melancholy kindness. 'I have missed you so much all through the day; a day which has been so sadly trying for your old friend. I have greatly suffered; suffered above all—I say it with humility—from the effort it has cost me to triumph over a bad feeling—over pride. Your uncle says that such combats are salutary when we come out of them victorious. He is right; but they bruise both body and mind.'

A little later, after having remained silent for some time, she suddenly said,

'You must naturally wish to know what it is that, for some time past, has caused me so much sorrow. Perhaps your uncle has spoken to you of it; has he?'

'Certainly not, madame. It would be impossible for my uncle to speak to me of secrets which are not his. Neither do I wish to know anything about them.'

'Alas, there is no secret, little one, but misery and shame, which are doubtless but too well known already. Since your uncle has been silent, however, I will myself tell you.'

'I prefer not to hear anything, madame.'

'If you have any affection for me, ought you not to desire to be made acquainted with my sorrows?'

'No, madame. It is sufficient for me to know that if I could do anything, however little it might be, to soften them, you would tell me.'

'You have already done much by coming to share my solitude, my poor child. But I would rather tell you everything. You must know then—'

'One moment, madame,' interrupted Mariette. 'As my uncle has not spoken to me of your trials, when, as you say, he might have done so, it is doubtless because he did not think it right I should be made acquainted with them.'

'Do you mean,' asked the old lady, with haughty bitterness, ' that the Marquise de Saissières could not speak of family misfortunes to Mademoiselle Marie de Reux without running the risk of wounding her ears ?'

'Pardon me!' Mariette eagerly replied. 'I had no intention whatever of offending you. Can you not understand my scruples? It is true that I ought to have remembered you could have nothing to say to me, madame, to which it would have been improper for me to listen. Once more I beg you to forgive me. I spoke without reflection, and like a child. Do not be hard upon me; and I entreat you not to call me by a name which recalls to me a time from which I am now so far removed. Let me be to you, as I am to every one else, Mariette—nothing more than little Mariette, the humble village Curé's poor little niece.'

The young girl uttered these last words with an emotion which touched the Marquise.

'I feel,' said she, taking her youthful companion's hand in hers, 'as though it were I who ought to ask pardon rather than you, since it is I who have wounded you. Yes, my dear child, I understand your scruples; they are proper and wise, as everything about you is. But since I must not speak to you of my sorrows, will you not speak to me of yours?'

'My sorrows, madame!—what sorrows? I have none.'

'It is impossible that, born in a rank so different from the one to which you are now reduced, you should not sometimes suffer, Mariette.'

'Yet so it is, madame.'

'How much I admire such resignation, and how greatly I envy it!'

'I do not deserve either admiration or envy, madame, nor do I wish to appear better than I am. I confess, to my shame, that the first few months I spent at the presbytery were painful enough. But what is there astonishing or meritorious in it, if, knowing my uncle as I do, and loving him as he deserves to be loved, I should now feel that I am happier in his house than I could possibly be anywhere else?'

'But—but your poverty, my child? I trust that the word has nothing in it which wounds you.'

'Absolutely nothing, madame,' said Mariette, smiling; 'for my uncle first taught me not to blush at poverty, and afterwards to love it. If that astonishes you, it is only because you do not know what it is to have a guide such as is my uncle. Had he not taken me in hand, I should have been full of faults.'

'And now you are full of virtues.'

'O, almost!' Mariette added, still smiling. 'No, no, madame; I know perfectly well that I am nothing more than a poor little negative being. And yet—must I be perfectly sincere? Well, then, I must confess that it is not without some slight satisfaction I compare the little creature I am now with the vain and foolish girl who in gone-by days was called Marie de Reux.'

'Neither vain nor foolish, but brilliant and intellectual, if I may be allowed to say so.'

'I adhere to what I said, "vain and foolish;" it is really what I was formerly.'

'Formerly! Would not people imagine you were speaking of a very distant past?'

'It is not so much the length of time, but the changes that have taken place in us, which separate us from gone-by days. Only two years have past since, struck by a blow which fell like a thunderbolt in the midst of the vanities and frivolities which filled my life,—an orphan without resources, not able to consider even the luxurious dresses I had been accustomed to wear as belonging to myself,—I was brought by my uncle to his poor little home. Yes, only two years have passed since then; but it would be as impossible for me to become once more the young girl I was then, as to bring back those two years which have fled.'

'Tell me, however, my child, what the catastrophe was which so entirely altered your position. I have never heard the exact details.'

'The story is a very simple one, madame. If you wish, I will relate it in two words.'

'Wherefore in two words only? On the contrary, tell me everything. It will do you good—unless, indeed, it should revive your sorrows.'

'With the exception of the remembrance of my father's death, I have no sad recollections connected with looking back to a past in which I have nothing to regret. I have no secret grief to dwell upon, or any sorrow which calls for sympathy. On the other hand, I shall perhaps be exposed, whilst relating my story, to the risk of allowing something to escape me which might, unconsciously to myself, seem to imply that my poor father was to blame.'

'Well, then, tell me nothing, you mysterious child!'

'Mysterious! Good heavens! I never dreamt I should lay myself open to such a charge! This, then, since you wish to hear it, is the history of our family. My father and my uncle became orphans very early in life, and were left without any fortune. There were contrasts in character between them, such as, I fancy, but rarely exist between brothers. The elder, my father, thought of nothing but the means of raising his family, and enabling it once more to occupy the rank whence it had been removed by poverty. My uncle, on the contrary, looking at life from a different point of view, submissively accepted the lot which it had pleased Providence to assign to him, and did not aspire to anything beyond a useful and busy life, no matter how lowly it might be. He entered the seminary. My father ceased to see him, and busied himself in trying one means after another whereby to make his fortune, met with partial success and married, spite of my mother bringing him but a very modest dowry. After two years of wedded life she died when giving birth to me. It was a terrible loss to my father, and he lavished upon me the whole of his affection. In his passionate tenderness he surrounded me with luxuries which were out of proportion to his means. In order to increase his fortune he embarked in hazardous speculations, which resulted in completely ruining him; and when death came and snatched him away, he left behind him nothing but creditors, whom it was impossible to satisfy. Beside myself with grief, there suddenly appeared at my father's deathbed the uncle whose name I had hardly ever heard pronounced, and who pressed me, weeping, to his heart. Taken to his home I soon became the

Mariette whom you see before you. That is the whole of my story, madame.'

'And you will not let me admire the courage with which you submitted to such a transformation?'

'No, madame,' said Mariette, smiling; 'you must not admire anything about me. If I am animated by any right and true feelings, if any sound principles have taken possession of my heart, the merit belongs to my uncle, and not in the least degree to myself. I shall always remember the first lesson which my dear good uncle gave me. Removed hurriedly from my father's house, of which his creditors were soon to take possession, I had wrapped myself, without thinking much of what I was doing, in a certain very costly cashmere shawl, the last gift of my poor father. As soon as I had reached the presbytery, I put on mourning, which was made in as simple a manner as possible; so simple, indeed, that only a little time before I should not have considered it suitable even for my maid; but I wore it without paying any attention to it. My uncle then spoke to me of the value of my cashmere shawl, and soon afterwards of my father's creditors, who were still clamouring for payment. Can you imagine, madame, that he was obliged often to return to the subject during several succeeding days before I was capable of understanding him? Alas, I had then so little heart! I ended, however, by discovering what he meant. The cashmere, my watch, and my rings were all sold, and the produce went to the creditors. "My child," said my uncle, "you have often heard your father repeat his favourite motto, 'Noblesse oblige.' Let us also take the same motto for ours; but let us attach to it another meaning, or rather— No, we will not speak of 'noblesse;' we will call it simply ' duty.'"'

Madame de Saissières, who had observed Mariette attentively whilst she had been relating her little story, said gently,

'I look upon your uncle as a quite incomparable man, and I certainly admit that he is capable of working miracles. But at the risk of annoying you, I must say that I do not put much faith in the one which you pretend has taken place in yourself?'

'What do you mean, madame?'

'Simply that you are resigned, but not in the least happy; and that careless Mariette is only a mask worn by sorrowful Marie de Reux.'

'A mask—O madame!'

'The word is absurd, I allow, when applied to you, darling; and I retract it at once. But this is what I think: you are suffering bravely, without wishing any one to pity you or even to know it. You assume a calmness, a serenity which you do not really possess. Never having betrayed yourself whilst acting your part, you have kept up a character for resignation even in your own eyes. In a word, my poor dear Mariette,—and this you must quite understand is entirely to your credit,—you are not *true !*'

Mariette bent down her head. After a moment's silence she said, in a voice which was rather agitated,

'Let us leave the subject, I beg of you, madame. If my cheerfulness be only on the surface, as you say, it is doubtless because my heart has not yet learnt submission. When we have not courage manfully to accept our lot in this world, it seems to me that we ought, at least, to exercise dignity, and not to utter any complaint. To be determined not to confess our sufferings is to prove that we consider them reprehensible. But now, madame, let us speak of yourself and of your sorrows. A little while ago you were going to tell me everything.'

'You have just given me a lesson in stoicism which has not been lost upon me. I do not desire to be pitied any more than you do.'

'That means that you wish me to understand I was very foolish to speak to you as I have done. I was doubtless under the influence of vanity without being aware of it, when—'

'You are a terrible child,' said the Marquise, with a smile. 'I certainly thought that you were possessed by one species of vanity, namely, that of being perfect, and even more than perfect. You have spoken only too well, and whilst listening to you I felt very much ashamed—I, full of worldly pride as I am still, at an age in which the world ought to have lost all attraction in one's eyes. Besides, I have no right to be as proud as you are. I am willing to receive pity, I am indeed; and it solaces my heart. Pity me, then! I am going to impart some of my sorrows to you. You know what grief the loss of my son occasioned me!—and yet, how should you know it? One must have passed through such trials in order to be able to understand them. How shall I find words whereby to describe to you my despair? Early left a widow, I made my only son the aim and object of my life. Ambitious in my tenderness, I desired that he should be as great in his career as he was by his birth; and I attained my wishes. His delicate health would have led him to prefer a tranquil life; but I stimulated and encouraged him, and he became inspired by the noble ambition of adding fresh lustre to the name he bore. Not content with having led him to devote his youth to the pursuits of studies which enabled him to become known very early in life by means of the works which he published, I had courage enough to resolve that he should serve his country with his sword. It was a terrible trial for me, my child; but by what a triumph was it not repaid? How happy it made me to have given birth to so noble a son! How proud I was of my work! A brilliant alliance, which I had long beforehand arranged for him, put the finishing stroke to my happiness.

'I would not permit my son's marriage to furnish him with a pretext for retiring from the army, and I made it a condition that he should still continue to pursue a career in which he had already gained so much glory. He did so. But his health gave way. An incurable languor took possession of him, and, by little and little, his strength deserted him. The premature death of his young wife was the last blow which completely overpowered my unhappy son. After two years of suffering he died in my arms. I should have died also if it had not been that he bequeathed his son to me as a legacy; and I had to recommence my task, as it were, on his behalf. I set myself to it with a courage inspired by despair. But what was my destined reward? Hardly had this son of my son attained the age of manhood before he escaped from my severe but legitimate control. I vainly attempted to awaken in him the feeling without which man is incomplete—ambition. He never possessed it.

'Endowed with brilliant talents, but thoughtless and greedy in the pursuit of pleasure, he found it impossible to follow the studious life which I had wished him to lead; and after a series of contests in which he displayed, spite of the puerility of his character, all the energy of his race, he left me to enter upon an existence more in harmony with his tastes. The law not giving me the means of exercising any salutary authority over him, there was nothing left for me to do in my mute and powerless indignation but to break off all intercourse with this unfortunate heir of so great a name.

'Two years passed away. Thanks to his patrimony, Gaston was independent. But I had kept in my own hands the power of leaving to whom I pleased the immense property which I possessed at the time of my marriage with his grandfather. The fortune which my grandson had inherited was soon spent; and, finding himself without resources, he has of late been obliged to have recourse to me. Although my heart remained closed to him, I did not wish to treat him with too great severity with regard to miserable money matters. Encouraged by my kindness, which he took for weakness, he suddenly dared to confess to me a design he had formed of giving his name—the name of his father, the name which I myself bear—to a wretched creature who had been the associate and accomplice of his vices. From that moment I ceased to acknowledge him, and forbade that any one should speak of him, or that his name should be mentioned in my presence. A whole year passed in this way. Imagine, my child, what I must have felt when, a few days ago, Gaston de Saissières, braving my prohibition, and transgressing my peremptory commands, appeared here at the château and dared to enter my apartments. I ought to have driven him away; but my strength failed me. Deceived by his hypocritical protestations,

I believed in his possible return to the paths of rectitude and honour. I consented that the culprit should remain for a time beneath the same roof as myself. I gave up to him the opposite wing of the château as his residence, and I sought the advice of your uncle as to the line of conduct it would be right for me to pursue. But what was my indignation on learning that Gaston was not alone when he arrived at the château! That detestable woman had followed him; he had permitted her to sully my dwelling by her presence; in his audacity he had installed her at the château, at the same time begging my servants to conceal from me the fresh insult which he had inflicted upon my house. These people, seeing in him their future master, obeyed him. Lambert alone had courage to acquaint me with the truth. Transported with righteous anger, I did not know to what extreme measures I might not have had recourse if your uncle had not restrained me. I have yielded to his advice, —to his authority, I may say, I who have never before recognised any authority superior to my own. But the violence I have been obliged to do to my feelings has almost cost me the loss of my reason. I fully believe that at times I have been mad. It was then that the good Curé proposed to send for you, dear child. It seems that in my illness I often pronounced your name. Since then he has consented, spite of the legitimate repugnance which he felt, to take upon himself, the painful mission of acting as an intermediary between my grandson and myself. After having in vain endeavoured to kindle some sparks of right feeling in the heart of this unhappy man, he has come to an arrangement—it is the right word to use—with him whereby the departure of these people from the château will be secured; and he also sent for my lawyer, as it appeared that I had some wretched accounts to settle. After making a bargain, the very thought of which causes the blood to mount to my brow, the price of my repose was decided. I have bought from this unworthy boy his promise never again to impose on me the torture of his presence. At the last moment I had some scruples, but I ended by triumphing over them. This very day all has been brought to a conclusion, signed, and sealed. The château is purged from its worthless inmates. Henceforth I shall be alone in the world. It signifies but little for the short remainder of my life.

'But enough! Let us try to think no more of all this villany; and as we have bought and paid for our repose, let us endeavour to enjoy it. Since you came here, Mariette, you have passed a sorrowful time. I wish that, for your sake, I could at least put on an appearance of cheerfulness.'

And the old lady began to speak with animation on subjects which she imagined were most likely to interest her young companion. But Mariette, fancying that she perceived symptoms of feverish agitation in her patient, begged she would retire to rest.

The Marquise consented to her proposal, but only on condition that Mariette would remain with her whilst she was undressing and preparing for the night. When her maids had left the room she put Mariette's arm very fondly within her own, and said,

'Come, child, I am going to show you into your little room. I want to delay going to bed myself as long as possible, for, to tell you the truth, it is only in order to obey you that I am going to lie down. I am certain that I shall not be able to sleep.'

So they walked together towards the young girl's room. Just when Mariette was about to open the door she was astonished to see the handle turn slowly; then the door opened, and the Marquis Gaston de Saissières appeared at it.

CHAPTER V.

SURPRISED, no doubt, at seeing the two ladies almost on the threshold, the Marquis paused. He was very pale, and the expression of his face was so sombre that Mariette, agitated by such a sudden and inexplicable apparition, was unable to repress a frightened cry. The Marquise, on her side, trembled so violently that she was nearly falling; but she remained absolutely mute, and drawing herself up to her full height, she made a step forward. The grandson and the grandmother fixed upon each other a gaze which was almost appalling.

After a moment's immobility the young man endeavoured to enter into the room. But the old lady, stretching out her arm, exclaimed, in a hollow voice,

'Leave me!'

The Marquis imperceptibly shrugged his shoulders.

'You will pardon me, madame,' he said, with apparent calm, but in an agitated tone,—'you will pardon me for having introduced myself into your rooms, spite of your commands, at such an hour as this. I must have an interview with you. You know it. I have desired you should be told. I have even written to you to that effect. You have thought it right to forbid me your door. Be it so. I can quite understand that my presence is disagreeable. I will not impose it upon you beyond the time which is strictly necessary for what I have to say to you. For *you must positively* listen to me. Resign yourself, then; I swear that I will be brief.'

Thus speaking, he gently led his grandmother towards an easy-chair, and inviting her, by a gesture, to be seated, he sat down himself.

'You will, of course, feel the propriety of retiring, mademoiselle,' he then said to the Curé's niece. 'What I have to say to Madame la Marquise must be heard by her alone. Pardon me for having ventured, in order to reach the rooms of the Marquise, to pass through the one which you are at present occupying. Thanks to the commands given by your uncle, all the doors were so carefully guarded that, if I had not remembered I could pass through your room, I should have been obliged, I believe, to have recourse to force. Accept, then, my excuses for my involuntary indiscretion, and lay it to the account of M. le Curé.'

Then by a gesture, which conveyed as clearly as possible to Mariette the intimation that she must at once withdraw, he gravely added,

'Good-evening, mademoiselle.'

The young girl cast an inquiring glance towards

the Marquise to ascertain whether she wished her to obey. Madame de Saissières looked fixedly at her grandson, and her black eyes darted fire from under their wrinkled lids. Standing upright before him, she seemed as though she would annihilate him with her anger and contempt.

'This, then,' she said slowly, and in a bitter tone, —'this, then, is the value to be henceforth attached to the promise made by a De Saissières! Scarcely a few hours back you entered on this very spot into an engagement by which you bound yourself on your honour to quit the château and never again to present yourself before my eyes; and now you come stealing furtively and insolently into my room, thereby casting contempt upon your plighted words! And yet you were paid for the promise which you gave! The cost was accurately counted out and handed over to you before my very eyes. I beheld that miserable hand pick up the bank-notes spread out before you. Do you pretend that one of them was deficient? You yourself counted them like a tradesman who wishes to be certain that he has received full value for the merchandise he is about to deliver up.'

'Madame,' interrupted Gaston, with affected calmness, 'permit me to stop you. The manner in which you have begun to speak leads me to fear that very soon we may both of us be tempted to overpass the bounds of moderation, within which, for my part at a rate, I desire to remain; and which well-born persons,' he added, accentuating the words, 'ought always to regard as a law.'

'Really!' exclaimed the Marquise contemptuously. 'And how long is it since you became acquainted with what well-born persons do or do not do? What is there in common, I should like to know, between them and you?'

'A strange question, indeed, to put to the son of your son!'

'Silence, unhappy man, and never utter again the name of your father! To allow it to proceed out of your mouth is to inflict a blot upon it.'

The Marquis involuntarily raised his eyelids, with a gesture which showed that it was not without an effort he restrained himself. Nevertheless he composedly answered,

'I have known for a long time past, madame, that you excel in the art of addressing insults to those whom you hate. I will not even allow myself to reply to you. Besides, do you not think that you could spare me a continuance of these amenities, and listen to what I am about to say?'

'What is there I can have to listen to from you? What fresh insult are you about to inflict upon me?'

'You are unjust, madame. I have never once forgotten to show you the respect which is your due. Whatever may have been your conduct, your harsh ness, your severity towards me, I have always maintained the deference—'

'What absurdity!' exclaimed Madame de Saissières bitterly. 'Do not add ridicule to insolence. The worst injuries you have done me are not those which proceed out of your mouth. Is the cynical calm with which—as, for example, at the present moment—you cast my authority to the winds, a merit in your eyes? In my opinion it is nothing more than the lowest degree of hypocrisy and hardness of heart.'

The young man made an involuntary movement, and seemed about to reply angrily. But passing his hand across his brow, as though he wished to efface from it every trace of annoyance,

'What would our intercourse have become, madame,' he asked, 'if for a long time past I had not been able to impose upon myself the moderation which you just now reproached me so bitterly for exercising? I have, it is true, liberated myself from the absolute authority which you attempted to wield over me. But my crime has not gone further.'

'That authority,' cried the Marquise, with vehemence, 'was just and necessary. By freeing yourself from it you were lost. Your crime, in order to make use of your own words, has not consisted in having attained your liberty, but in having made a most shameful use of it. What sort of life has yours been since you escaped from me? Tell me if you dare.'

'To refer to the past would, it seems to me, be useless, madame. It is the present, or rather the future, that is to be the subject of our conversation.'

'Good heavens! what can you have to say to me about a future which will doubtless behold you dishonouring for ever the name of your father by giving it to a—'

'Silence, madame!' exclaimed the young man, in a trembling voice. 'Let your insults be inflicted on me alone. I will not suffer them to go beyond that limit.'

'You will not *suffer* them!' repeated the Marquise slowly, and with a contemptuous laugh. 'You will not *suffer* them! And if it pleases me—*me*, do you hear?—to characterise the audacious adventuress as she deserves—'

'It is too much!' cried the Marquis, rising with so much impetuosity that he overthrew a table standing before him. 'You are making too great an abuse, madame, of your age, of your sex, of the consideration which I owe to the mother of my father.'

The Marquise advanced a couple of steps towards her grandson.

'Never has there yet been a man, before you, who has dared to raise his voice when speaking to me, and still less to abandon himself, in my presence, to violence of the grossest kind, and of which this piece of furniture you have just thrown down is the witness. Do you think that you will frighten me, sir? In that case you are deceived. If you forget yourself, I have people about me who will drive you away. It has pleased me to say, and it pleases me to repeat, that this woman is a vile adventuress. Do not oblige me to add that he who loves her is a wretch.'

Ever since this scene had commenced, Mariette, not daring to interfere, had nevertheless hesitated to withdraw. After having vainly endeavoured to attract the attention of the Marquise for a moment, she went towards the door leading into her room, and there remained, divided between the wish to hear nothing more and the fear of leaving her old friend alone with her grandson. At length she was about noiselessly to quit the room, ready to reappear at the first summons or appearance of her presence being required, when Madame de Saissières, suffocated by grief and indignation, turned pale, tottered, and fell backwards upon a sofa, seized by a violent spasm.

Mariette ran to her, and when the Marquis, casting aside his borrowed calmness, prepared once more to speak, she said to him, in a decided tone,

'In the name of Heaven, sir, withdraw. Do you not see that all this agitation is killing her?'

After having twice paced up and down the room with a hasty step, Gaston, without uttering a word, went out by the door of the picture-gallery.

Mariette, frightened by the state into which the Marquise had fallen, was about to ring for her maids, when Madame de Saissières, guessing at her intention, made her a sign not to do so. As soon as she was able to speak,

'I do not wish to have any one but you with me,' she stammered. 'Do not be afraid, I shall be better immediately.'

In fact, she soon began to breathe more freely. For some moments she remained motionless, her eyebrows contracted, and murmuring angry words; then she covered her face with both her hands and cried bitterly.

'Be of good heart, madame!' exclaimed Mariette, who was kneeling before her. 'Courage has never failed you yet. Did you not tell me so?'

'I am wounded to the quick,' answered the Marquise, in a broken voice. 'It is my death they desire. They will not have to wait much longer for it. You were there, little one; you saw him, you heard him. Have I had sufficient outrages inflicted upon me? Of what effrontery, of what cruelty has not this boy been guilty! What did he wish? Doubtless it was to see me fall down dead at his feet.'

'Do not allow yourself to indulge in such thoughts, madame. They will only serve to embitter your grief; besides which there is nothing to authorise you to give way to them.

'Nothing which authorises me, you say? But when he saw me stretched upon the sofa, my strength gone from me, and hardly able to breathe, did he show the very slightest symptom of pity for me? Did he not leave me at once?'

'I was at hand to give you aid, madame. Besides, M. de Saissières was not sufficiently calm and master of himself just then to be aware of what was going on around him.'

'You are in the wrong, child. That cold hard heart is ignorant of all emotions. Do you know that I have never received from my grandson one single word of affection?'

Mariette looked at the Marquise with some astonishment, and could not prevent herself from remarking that she thought Madame de Saissières had always claimed much more of submission than of affection from the Marquis.

'I desired to have both the one and the other,' said the old lady hotly. 'Submission first, because I possessed the energy and judgment which were deficient in my grandson's weak nature; affection afterwards, because it was due to me, and because I had a right to it, an absolute right. What have you to object, child? You are shaking your head.'

'Pardon me, madame, I said nothing.'

'No, but I observed an involuntary gesture. You seem to think that I had no right to the affection of a child for whom I did so much! Speak, what is your opinion?'

'I was simply asking myself, madame, in what *rights to affection* really consist. Affection, it seems to me, is given, and not imposed.'

The Marquise started, and seemed about to make an impetuous answer; but she restrained herself. Her features became relaxed, her tears flowed anew, and letting her head fall upon her breast, she murmured,

'You are, perhaps, right, my child. It may be that I have sometimes been too severe. But my intentions have always been good. I have, most probably, a haughty temperament, but I have not a cold heart. There are moments even now, when, however great has been my righteous anger, some few affectionate words would have been sufficient to disarm me. But there has been nothing, nothing, nothing! I shall die alone and desolate. O, that the end may come quickly!'

Whilst speaking, Madame de Saissières' voice became weaker and weaker, until she fell into a state of prostration, out of which Mariette was utterly unable to rouse her. The Curé's niece was all the more anxious because it was such a contrast to the almost masculine energy which the Marquise exhibited on all occasions.

Alarmed at the responsibility which weighed upon

her, Mariette resolved to summon her uncle and the doctor. But it was late; she would have to call up the servants, and it would take a long time before the Curé and the physician could reach the château. Meanwhile the Marquise seemed to become more and more exhausted. Lying upon the sofa, her eyes half closed, she reclined in the arms of Mariette, and from time to time feebly murmured the name of her grandson. Conjecturing what the sad results of such an attack might be in the case of a person of the age of Madame de Saissières, Mariette felt that it was necessary she should do something at once. With her usual promptness she resolved that she would inform the young Marquis of what had occurred, and, if it were possible, induce him to come to his grandmother. But if she sent for him by a servant, would he obey the summons? And if he did consent, would he come into the room in such a frame of mind that a single harsh or unkind word might cost Mariette's patient her life? She felt as though, could she but speak to the young man herself for one moment, she would be able to address to him words which would enable her to bring him back repentant to her whom he had offended. A very natural idea, doubtless, but ascending from a warm heart to a head which was still young and to which present anxieties did not allow space for cool reflection. Mariette, therefore, hastily resolved to go herself in search of Gaston. She rang the bell. Lambert answered it, followed by Madame de Saissières' maids. Confiding the Marquise to their care, she inquired where the young Marquis was to be found. Lambert having told her with a sigh that he was still at the château, she desired the old servant to take her at once to him. He looked at her with surprise; but the young girl having impatiently repeated her orders, adding that she was acting in the name of the Marquise, he immediately obeyed.

It was necessary that they should traverse almost the whole of the vast and sombre château in order to reach that portion of the building which the Marquise had assigned to her grandson.

'This is the apartment occupied by M. le Marquis Gaston,' said Lambert, pausing before a closed door. 'Unless mademoiselle positively commands me to do so, I will not enter it. You will, however, find M. le Marquis's valet in the anteroom.'

'Very well,' answered Mariette, without giving herself time for reflection; 'wait for me here.'

She then entered the anteroom, and found herself in the presence of two valets, who were reclining upon easy-chairs; and in one of whom she recognised the servant she had seen the night of her arrival at the château.

'I wish to speak to your master at once,' she said hastily.

'Ah,' he exclaimed, looking at her with curiosity,

F

and without rising from his seat, 'what do you want with him, if you please?'

'I will tell him myself when I see him,' replied the young girl, full of her strange enterprise. 'Call him immediately.'

'Call him, indeed! At what a pace you are going, my dear! Do you imagine that M. le Marquis is accustomed to come the moment he is summoned?'

'Beg him, then, to receive me,' went on Mariette, with difficulty restraining her impatience.

'I would just as soon a wolf should crack my bones. I am not going to do it. M. le Marquis is in there,' he continued, pointing to a door. 'He is not alone. He has forbidden any one to enter, and I will not go in.'

'You will—you must!'

'Indeed! In order, I suppose, that he may make me leave the room by the window, to teach me obedience? Thank you for your kind proposal. I am not going to stir.'

'You must obey me!' exclaimed Mariette, with severity. 'I come here commissioned by Madame la Marquise.'

The valet reflected for a moment; then, turning towards his companion, he said, in a whisper,

'Do you hear? What shall I do?'

'Since she has been sent by the old lady,' replied the other, in the same tone, 'I think you may as well tap at the door. But you incur the chance of coming in for a box on the ear if he is in one of his bad tempers; and yet, if you refuse, you run the risk of being dismissed.'

The valet rose and in a hesitating manner went and tapped at the door which he had pointed out to Mariette. He did so several times without receiving any answer. The Curé's niece could hardly restrain herself. She was just going to knock, when a man's voice at last called out,

'Come in.'

'Wait where you are,' said the valet, and he disappeared, carefully closing the door behind him. Five minutes passed, and then he returned.

'You can go in,' he said, standing on one side to allow Mariette to pass.

CHAPTER VI.

THE Curé's niece entered boldly into a drawing-room that was brilliantly illuminated, and the atmosphere of which was laden with delicate perfumes, recalling to Mariette's remembrance her former years of luxury. A young and beautiful woman was standing near a table, on which were spread the remains of a repast. The lady, after casting upon Mariette a glance of curiosity and examining her well, said, in a gently modulated voice,

'Come forward, mademoiselle.'

Then addressing herself to a man who was seated at the table, with his elbow resting upon it, in the midst of a set of glasses, and his head bowed upon his hands, 'I will leave you,' she said to him.

And slowly crossing the room she disappeared. The Curé's niece, thinking only of the mission with which she was charged, advanced towards the man, whose face she could not see.

'I am come for you, M. le Marquis. Your grandmother is dying,' she hastily exclaimed.

'Indeed!' answered an unknown voice. 'These

are important tidings which you have brought, mademoiselle!'

And the man, raising his head, exhibited to Mariette features which were completely unknown to her. Seized with astonishment, the young girl stepped back.

'I had imagined,' she said, 'that I was speaking to M. le Marquis Gaston de Saissières.'

'Yes, I thought so,' replied the unknown, smiling. 'Gaston will be here in a moment. Sit down, mademoiselle, I beg. Is Madame la Marquise so very ill?'

'I beg your pardon, monsieur,' Mariette answered. 'I am in a hurry—time presses. I must speak at once to M. de Saissières.'

'He is coming, mademoiselle; he has been sent for. Sit down, I beg.'

Mariette refused by a gesture.

'Has Madame de Saissières been ill long? Is it something serious?'

'Yes,' answered Mariette briefly. 'It is absolutely necessary that her grandson should go to her at once.'

'Has she asked for him? Does she wish to speak to him? He did not see her this evening, I think, did he? You have been constantly with the Marquise, have you not, mademoiselle?'

Mariette bowed without making any answer.

'Madame de Saissières has of course spoken to you,' he continued, 'of her grandson, and of certain differences which have risen between him and her.

Now what are her real feelings towards Gaston? She loves him, does she not? It is only by way of a threat, surely, that she speaks of making him leave the château? What has she said to you respecting her intentions?'

'Madame de Saissières has not confided anything to me,' the young girl replied very calmly; 'and if she had done so it would have been impossible for me, monsieur, to have replied to the question you have put to me.'

'I understand,' said the stranger. 'You do not know who I am. You see in me, mademoiselle, the most intimate friend, the confidant—I might almost the *mentor*—of Gaston. I have rendered services to him which would hardly leave him the right of despising my advice, if he were ever inclined to do so.'

'Monsieur,' said Mariette, as if she had not even heard a syllable of what he had been saying, 'time presses, and M. de Saissières does not make his appearance. I am going to speak to the valet who brought me in here.'

'It is useless, mademoiselle. I have the honour to repeat to you for the third time that Gaston is coming. He has been informed that you are here. Have patience, and wait a few moments longer. It will not be useless, perhaps, that you and I should have a short conversation together. I know well what is the influence which your uncle and you, mademoiselle, exercise over Madame de Saissières. On my side, I have just told you that there is *nothing* I cannot do with her grandson. By uniting our efforts we shall soon be able, I think, to put an end to these unhappy divisions. It is on this subject that I wish to speak to you now that the opportunity presents itself. I will tell you frankly what it is which we must obtain from the old lady. In your turn, you shall tell me what little concessions it will be necessary the young man should make.'

'I regret not to be able to listen to you, monsieur. It is impossible for me to accede to your wishes.'

'That is very strange, mademoiselle. It is impossible that you should take no interest whatever in a matter which touches your patroness so very closely. Have you no affection for her, then?'

Surprised and displeased by the species of interrogation to which she was being subjected, Mariette raised her eyes towards her interlocutor, and met a piercing and fixed gaze, which disconcerted her in spite of herself. She would have wished, if not to suppress her displeasure, at any rate to show it only by her silence, but involuntarily she answered,

'I feel for Madame de Saissières all the affection which she so well deserves. Nevertheless—'

She paused.

'Prove your affection, then, by rendering a signal service to her who is the object of it.'

'I cannot see that there is a possibility of my rendering her any service whatever. Humble devotion is all that she can expect me to give her.'

'You speak like a child, Listen to me. You are aware of what has taken place at the château during the last few days?'

'I do not know, and I ought not to know, anything,' Mariette hastily answered.

'That is also very strange. No matter. You are at any rate aware that, on account of her obstinate and unjustifiable refusal to consent to her grandson's marriage, the old lady has driven him beyond all bounds; and that your uncle—'

'I will not listen to anything more, monsieur,' said the young girl. 'Whilst I am lingering here she of whom you speak is, perhaps, in need of my services. I must return to her. Since I cannot see M. Gaston de Saissières, I beg you to tell him, monsieur, that his grandmother is very ill, and that I entreat him—that is to say, I believe that if he would but address a few affectionate words to her—'

'If I desire Gaston to go to his grandmother, he will do so,' said the unknown; 'and he will speak to her in the manner I shall prescribe.'

'Make him come at once, then, monsieur,' said Mariette, going towards the door; 'and if, thanks to your advice, the expressions of which he will make use should be those of affection and submission, you will have performed a good work.'

'I will speak to Gaston only on condition that you, on your side, will speak to the Marquise in the manner I have indicated.'

'I cannot take upon myself any such communication, monsieur. Besides, Madame de Saissières is not in a state to receive any message at present.'

'Very well. But she will recover her composure, and then—'

'Excuse me, monsieur. If you have any advice to give to Madame de Saissières, speak to my uncle, or any one else whom you may think proper. Allow me to withdraw.'

Bowing slightly, Mariette was about to leave the room when she found that the door was fastened outside. She turned and cast a questioning glance upon the stranger, who said, in a careless tone,

'You are wrong to be resolved neither to help nor to listen to me. You will regret it. You are assuming a heavy responsibility. The frame of mind you are manifesting has made me resolve not to permit a fresh interview to take place between my friend and his grandmother.'

'I can neither understand nor allow such language to be used towards me,' said Mariette, in an agitated tone. 'In what way my frame of mind can have any influence over the conduct of M. de Saissières, or the intentions of Madame de Saissières, I am absolutely at a loss to comprehend, monsieur, or why it should please you to attribute to me an influence I do not possess, and to which I cannot and will not lay claim.'

'I know better, perhaps, than you do the extent of your influence over Madame de Saissières. In any case, if you do not possess it, you can obtain it; and I will tell you how to employ it on behalf of every one concerned, including yourself.'

These last words restored to Mariette the calmness which she had somewhat lost.

'Our interview, monsieur,' she said, 'will not be productive of any beneficial result, and I desire that it should come to an end. The door is locked, I find. Will you have the goodness to desire it may be opened?'

'Is it really locked? Yes, it is probable it may be. But, after all, it is not of much consequence, for you will be obliged to await Gaston's arrival.'

'I have given up the idea of appealing to him, monsieur. You will be sure to acquaint him with his grandmother's state?'

'On the contrary, I will say nothing to him, and I will, moreover, take care that he hears nothing. You are aware of my conditions!'

'Your conditions! I will not even attempt to understand you, monsieur.'

'Yet I have expressed myself very clearly. I offer to use my influence over Gaston, but I expect you to exercise yours over the Marquise.'

Without appearing to understand what he meant, Mariette said aloud,

'I will send M. de Saissières word by one of the servants. It is what I ought to have done in the first instance. I cannot believe that he will refuse to come to his grandmother.'

'No, not if I allow him to do so,' replied the other, with a sardonic laugh.

Without deigning to answer, the young girl once more attempted to open the door. Not being able to succeed, she knocked and called out. No one replied.

'Monsieur,' she impetuously exclaimed, 'I beg of you to desire that the door shall be opened!'

'What can I do that you have not done, mademoiselle? You have knocked, and called out, and you see that no one answers.'

'Is there no bell, monsieur?'

'There is absolutely none, mademoiselle. We are miserably off for everything in this part of the château. I have already said so to Gaston more than once.'

And so speaking, the stranger ensconced himself comfortably in his easy-chair, as though he had resolved to take no more notice of Mariette. She profited by his position in order to examine him hastily. He was still young and of aristocratic appearance. His features were regular and even handsome, but the equivocal expression of his eyes and of his mouth inspired a feeling of distrust and repulsion. The young girl felt that her position was an extraordinary one. Endowed with much self-control and decision of character; possessed, moreover, of the self-reliance which intercourse with the world produces, but which was hardly to be looked for in so young a girl springing from the class to which Mariette seemed to belong, she fancied that an endeavour was being made to intimidate her, and wishing to show that it had not succeeded,

'All this, monsieur,' she dryly observed, 'gives me the idea of its being a pleasantry of which, I confess, I neither understand the appropriateness nor the good taste. You do not, I suppose, intend to keep me here, in spite of my wishes to the contrary?'

'O, certainly not, mademoiselle.'

'Then why is the door locked?'

'I do not know. It is, perhaps, a piece of carelessness on the part of the servant who brought you into the room.'

'Make him unlock it, then!'

'I will willingly try, mademoiselle. Perhaps I shall be more fortunate than you.'

The stranger rose, went to the door, shook it, knocked, and called out very conscientiously; but it was all of no avail.

'You see, mademoiselle,' he said, seating himself once more; 'it is very provoking, but what can I do? And now, since you are obliged to wait until Gaston comes to set you at liberty—for he will, doubtless, be able to make his servants open the door—you can have nothing better to do than to sit down and listen to what I have to say: I shall not keep you long.'

'I will not wait a moment longer, monsieur. My place is beside Madame de Saissières, whom I ought not to have left.'

'That is possible; it is even probable, mademoiselle; but I do not at all see how it will be practicable for you immediately to return to her.'

'I will leave by one of those doors,' said Mariette, pointing resolutely towards two doors which she saw at the other end of the room.

'Certainly it is one way of getting out of this room, but not of reaching the apartments of Madame de Saissières. One of those doors leads into the room belonging to my sister, the young lady who was here a moment ago; the other opens into the chamber which Gaston and I occupy. But, thanks to the clumsiness displayed by the architect, who was more or less Gothic in his tastes, and who planned this old building, there is no other way of reaching the principal portion of the house than the one by which you entered, mademoiselle; that is to say, by that door, that wretched door which has been locked in so absurd a fashion.'

Mariette reflected for a moment. She would not even admit that it was possible she could be exposed to any danger whatever beneath the roof of Madame de Saissières. Yet it was becoming quite evident that she was a prisoner, and that the drawing-room door had been intentionally locked, probably by order of her interlocutor. What grievance could this strange personage have against her? So much at home as he was in the apartments occupied by Gaston de Saissières, it was impossible to suspect him of any evil designs. But a thought suddenly presented itself to Mariette's mind which immediately caused her to tremble. Was she not being kept from the Marquise in order that Madame de Saissières might be subjected, without any possibility of interference, to importunities, to violence, perhaps even to— Mariette shuddered. Why, O why, had she ever quitted the patient who had been confided to her care? Was this what she had promised her uncle? What a ridiculous and romantic idea, on her part, to have imagined for a moment that it would be possible for her to induce the Marquis to betake himself to his grandmother! How could she have forgotten herself to such a degree as to quit the only post she was expected to fill, namely, that of sick-nurse and companion? Was she not aware that it was often as wrong to go beyond one's duty as to fall short of it? These reflections passed through her mind in a few seconds.

'Monsieur,' she exclaimed all at once, 'it was by your orders that this door has been locked! You wished, doubtless, to make me feel that my proper place is not here, and that I ought never to have left Madame de Saissières. The lesson has not been lost upon me. Do not prolong it, I entreat you!'

'I do not understand, mademoiselle, what lesson I could possibly have wished to give you. Be so good as to explain yourself.'

'It is useless, monsieur. Whatever may have been your intention, allow me to withdraw.'

'You have seen, mademoiselle, that I am powerless. No one answers when I call.'

'Monsieur, this is becoming a puerile and cruel joke. What do you want with me? If you will not reply, I will summon some one here by my cries.'

'But there is nothing I wish for more than to reply to you, mademoiselle. Remember, it is you who would not listen to me. If you had done so at first you would have doubtless been once more by this time with your old friend, and exercising your influence over her, whilst I was myself speaking to Gaston.'

In spite of her aversion, Mariette suddenly determined to allow the stranger to explain himself, as regarded the nature of the interference to which it was expected she should have recourse. It was doubtless the only means by which she could immediately recover her liberty; and if he indulged in language such as was not fit for her to hear, she would always be able to stop him.

'Speak, then,' she said; 'I am listening. But remember that you promised me to be brief, and that you are to open the door for me as soon as I have heard all.'

And again she refused, by a gesture, the chair which the unknown advanced towards her. Without pressing her to be seated, he thus addressed her, in a clear and concise manner:

'I will go straight to the object I have in view. Madame de Saissières has set herself, without the shadow of a reason, and with the most incredible obstinacy, against the marriage of her grandson with my sister. When I say she is opposing it, I speak incorrectly. It does not depend on her to prevent a marriage which is certain to take place, because it ought, and because I am resolved that it shall. But she will not give her consent, and she is determined to punish her grandson for what she styles his disobedience, by depriving him of a portion of the fortune which he expects to receive at her hands. This is what I cannot permit. I have allowed Gaston to make some ridiculous temporary arrangement or other with his grandmother, which obliges him, in consideration of a certain sum of money paid down to him, to quit the château immediately, and not to return to it during the lifetime of the Marquise. I consented to this because the young man was in money difficulties, from which he will be able to extricate himself by means of the sum handed over to him by Madame de Saissières. But I will not allow my future brother-in-law to be driven away, as it were, from the château under any pretext whatever. Having made an arrangement with him, Madame la Marquise has now to settle with me. She is ignorant that her grandson is dependent upon me; that I can compromise and dishonour him; and that I will do so without mercy, unless she accept my conditions. This, then, mademoiselle, is what I beg you to tell her from me. I had wished to have recourse to your uncle, but I found him so—unreasonable (I will spare you a harsher term), that I gave up the idea of asking him to use his influence, reserving to myself, however, the power of making him feel, if he should still dare to oppose me, the danger to which a priest exposes himself by interfering in family affairs. These, then, are my conditions: I desire that my sister should become the Marquise Gaston de Saissières, and that the marriage should take place before the end of the month; I demand that she should be accepted or received as such by the Dowager Marquise, and that this château should be her home; I require that Madame de Saissières should bind herself to leave the whole of her fortune to her grandson; and lastly, I desire that she should promise me a welcome here whenever it shall please me to visit this house. You are, perhaps, surprised, mademoiselle, that I should express myself in such peremptory terms. I have the right to do so, because I have the power to insist on my desires being carried out. Although not fully acquainted with the nature and extent of the engagements which her grandson has contracted with me, Madame de Saissières knows enough to comprehend the manner in which I ought to be treated. I believe she has been induced to think that I am satisfied with the arrangements made to-day. It is necessary she should be undeceived in this respect; and it is for you to perform that office, mademoiselle, since you, better than any one else, will be able to make that haughty woman listen to what you have to say. Relate to her, therefore, I request, our conversation. By doing so, you will render her a signal service. You will spare her the grief of beholding for ever dishonoured that name of which she is so proud, the name of De Saissières. Do you think it would be possible for her to survive such a humiliation? You well know that she could not. It is, therefore, her life which is in your hands. Make her comprehend the necessity of submission. In order that you may quite understand to what your old friend would expose herself by resisting me, it is perhaps necessary I should enter into some details.'

'Stop, monsieur,' said Mariette firmly. 'I will hear nothing more; and I desire that you will permit me to leave the room without any further delay.'

'Tell me first that you have understood the terms in which you must express yourself to the Marquise, and that you will do what is expected from you.'

'I will tell you nothing of the kind, monsieur,' answered the young girl, with intrepidity. 'I have of course understood that it is intended to constrain Madame de Saissières to a culpable submission to your demands, and that it is wished I should be the instrument whereby it is to be brought about. I will not repeat to the Marquise one single word respecting the conversation which has taken place between us this evening, but I will at once give an account of it to my uncle.'

'You will do nothing of the kind,' exclaimed the stranger, rising abruptly and casting upon Mariette a threatening glance.

'I will,' she answered boldly, 'I will; and since you persist in keeping the door locked, I will have it opened in spite of you.'

Carried away by her indignation, she began to knock loudly, and over and over again, at the door, calling out for Lambert and for all the servants at the château.

The stranger rushed towards her, and seizing her

by the wrist, 'Silence, fool!' he said, in a low voice, 'silence!'

Whilst endeavouring to disengage herself, Mariette involuntarily allowed an agonised scream to escape her. Retaining her by one hand, the unknown was about to lay his other upon her mouth, when suddenly he was whirled round; then he stumbled and fell backwards, and Mariette beheld before her the Marquis Gaston de Saissières. It was he whose unexpected interference had thus set her free. His arms crossed upon his breast, he gazed angrily at the stranger.

'George,' he exclaimed, 'what does this mean?'

'Great heavens!' cried George, slowly advancing towards him, 'is it really you, Gaston, who have dared to lay hands upon me?'

'Yes, it is I. What were you doing to the child?'

'I was preventing the little fool from crying out. Besides, what does it matter to you? and what are you doing here? I did not summon you. Return to your room.'

'I will not allow any violence to be used, George.'

'You will not allow it!—really! And for how long a time past have you been accustomed to speak to me in such a tone? Besides, there is no question of violence. Let the girl be silent, and listen to what there remains for me to say. As to you, I tell you once more to return to your apartment.'

Gaston seemed to hesitate.

'In the name of Heaven,' exclaimed Mariette, approaching Gaston, 'let me leave the room; and do you desire the door to be opened?'

'Why is the door locked, George?' asked the Marquis.

'Because it is my wish that it should be, and it shall not be opened except by my orders,' answered George.

'What do you mean? Do you forget that you are in my house?' asked the young man, drawing himself up.

'In your house!' replied the other, with a contemptuous laugh. 'And for how long a time has this château been yours? Besides, allowing that you are in your own house, it is only an additional reason for my being obeyed. I, in my turn, may well ask, do you forget that— Leave the room, I repeat, and do not irritate me any further!'

'I will not stir until you have permitted this young girl to withdraw.'

'Take care,' said George angrily, through his closed teeth; 'take care! You know that I am not endowed with patience.'

And, so saying, he laid his hand upon the shoulder of Gaston, who, spite of the efforts he made to free himself, appeared obliged to yield to the pressure, as though both his physical and moral powers were about to fail him. But perceiving that Mariette was looking anxiously at him, the young Marquis seemed ashamed of his weakness, and endeavouring to steady his voice,

'It is useless,' he said. 'I have told you that I will not move from here.'

'We must put a stop to all this,' said the other imperiously.

And he attempted to drag Gaston by force towards the other end of the room.

'M. le Marquis,' exclaimed Mariette, 'your grandmother is very ill; she wants me. Are you going to leave me here?'

'No,' he answered, making a violent effort to escape George's grasp.

But retaining his hold without any difficulty, the unknown rudely pushed Gaston, after a momentary struggle, towards the door by which he had entered. In striving to set himself free, he came in contact with the doorway, and striking his forehead against it, inflicted a slight wound whence blood flowed. As soon as George saw what had happened, he paused. Quick as thought the Marquis managed to slip out of his grasp, and seizing a sword-case that was lying upon a chair, he drew out of it a long and sharp blade, which whistled as he brandished it backwards and forwards.

'Touch me,' he murmured, grinding his teeth together, 'touch me again, and I kill you!'

Horrified, Mariette was just about to cast herself between the two combatants, when the young lady whom she had seen on first entering the room suddenly reappeared. Going straight up to Gaston, she snatched the sword out of his hands, passed her arm through his, and then, turning towards her brother,

'What does all this signify?' she asked, with her melodious voice.

Neither of the two men replied. Mariette, who was more desirous than ever to withdraw, and who dreaded being obliged to be present at any explanations, advanced with trembling steps.

'Madame, I entreat you to allow me to leave the room,' she said.

'Do you hear, George? Do what the child wants.'

'No, indeed! She must first promise—'

'I tell you, George, that you must let her leave the room at once, since she wishes to do so.'

'You are mad.'

'It is possible. Do, however, as I tell you.'

'Very well; I will obey you. But first take away the insane young man whom you are holding by the arm, and leave me alone for a moment with mademoiselle; I have one last word to say to her; afterwards she shall be set at liberty, I promise you.'

'I desire to leave the room at once,' exclaimed Mariette. 'Whatever it may be that you have to say, I will not listen to it. Madame, I conjure you, let me go!'

'Calm yourself,' said the beautiful unknown, with the tone of a queen promising her protection. 'George, desire the door to be unlocked. Do you hear me?'

'You will repent it,' murmured George, going towards the door. 'Anything to equal your stupidity—'

'Or your cleverness!' interrupted the young lady, with a sarcastic laugh. 'We have proof of it before us. But after all it is of no consequence. Open the door; I desire you to do so.'

In spite of his manifest and angry repugnance George knocked at the door in a peculiar manner, saying, in a half whisper, 'It is I; unlock the door;' on which it was immediately thrown open by the valet who had introduced Mariette into the drawing-room. With a hurried bow she escaped, as a bird would do on seeing the door of his cage opened, crossed the antechamber, and entered the vestibule where she had left Lambert. But he was no longer there. Overcome by the excitement she had just gone through, and thinking only of the Marquise, the young girl made her way, as well as she could through the darkness, to the portion of the château occupied by Madame de Saissières.

She had, at any rate, the comfort of finding her sleeping quietly, and of learning that no one had attempted to enter her room. When Mariette reproached Lambert with having quitted the antechamber without waiting for her to return from the apartments occupied by the Marquis, the old man informed her that a valet had come to tell him he was not to stay, as M. Gaston was himself going to take the young lady back to the Marquise. These tidings were a new subject of surprise to the Curé's niece. Vainly she endeavoured to seek the meaning of them in the strange drama which had but just been enacted. But of what nature soever might be the explanation, all that Mariette had seen and heard was sufficient to make her fear—in the same degree as she had, a little while back, longed—to see the young Marquis make his appearance in the apartment occupied by his grandmother. Agitated by indefinable fears and unable to seek refuge in slumber, she passed the remainder of the night beside her old friend. Day dawned without Gaston having shown himself, and without his having sent any one to inquire in his name after Madame de Saissières. This proof of indifference caused Mariette entirely to lose all opinion of him, and she waited impatiently for the Curé to come, that she might ask him if there was nothing which could be done in order to deliver the poor old lady from her persecutors. But it was too early for her to be able to send a message to the presbytery. The Marquise still slept. Mariette felt as though her brain were on fire, and overcome though she was by fatigue, she was forced to struggle against a nervous excitement which rendered it impossible for her to sit still. Trusting that the morning air would restore her to some degree of composure, she desired that she should be called as soon as the Marquise awoke, told Lambert to keep a careful watch, and locking the door of her own room, so that no one might pass through it, she descended by a private staircase into the enclosure where she had been wont to take a short walk every day.

After having paced up and down for some time, with a step which she involuntarily quickened under the influence of the fever which was already beginning to make her temples throb, she was suddenly seized with a lassitude which obliged her to seat herself upon a bench. The cold damp air seemed, little by little, to deprive her of all energy. She shivered several times, and felt that it was a warning to her to return to the château; but her strength failed her. Leaning her head on the back of the bench, she was overcome by insurmountable drowsiness; and soon afterwards fell into a slumber which was almost painful, it was so agitated. She very soon awoke under the impression of a frightful dream, which reproduced all the scenes she had witnessed the preceding night. Opening her eyes, she fancied for a moment that her dream was not yet over; for she beheld the Marquis Gaston standing motionless in front of her bench, and gazing at her with a serious countenance. Overwhelmed with confusion she rose.

'I am disturbing you, mademoiselle,' he said. 'Pardon me. I did not imagine I was guilty of indiscretion in following you hither. I have come from my grandmother's rooms, and am told that she is still asleep. Lambert would not allow me to enter her chamber. I submitted to the prohibition, and all the more easily because, to tell you the truth, it is you whom I wished to see. I was told that I should find you in the garden. Will you be so good as to listen to me, mademoiselle?'

'Listen to you, M. le Marquis,' said Mariette coldly: 'what can you have to say to me?'

'You will know immediately if you will only listen for a few moments.'

'The recollection of what took place last night makes me a little dread, I must confess, the conversation which you appear to desire. If it is any communication which you wish me to make—as it is but natural to suppose—to Madame de Saissières, it would be certainly better that it should not reach her through my mouth.'

'I understand your hesitation, mademoiselle; but it is precisely respecting what took place last night that I wish to speak to you.'

'I should prefer not to have any mention made of it between us, M. le Marquis.'

'I would have you observe, mademoiselle,' said Gaston, 'that there are no locked doors here; that no one has any intention of forcing you to hearken to me; and that you are simply requested to have the goodness to listen. You shake your head. Well, I will not insist. Permit me only to assure you that I had nothing to do with what I may call the snare into which you were momentarily drawn. Whatever may have been said to you about me, believe me, there are certain things of which I am incapable. And now, mademoiselle, I am about to beg you to give me your advice. You cannot refuse, because it is my grandmother who is in question. I am going to leave the château immediately. Shall I see Madame de Saissières before my departure, or will it be better that I should abstain from visiting her?'

'It is very difficult for me to answer such a question,' said Mariette, hesitating.

'You alone can reply, mademoiselle, because you alone are aware of what my grandmother's wishes really are with regard to this matter.'

'I cannot admit that it is incumbent on me to advise you, monsieur. Yet,' she added, seeing that the young man was about to insist on an answer, 'why should I be afraid of telling you that Madame de Saissières is exceedingly unhappy; that I beheld her yesterday weeping bitterly after you had left her; and that her poor wounded heart stands in great need of consolation? Can you bring it to her? If so, do not delay. If, however, on the contrary, you cannot pour any balm upon her wounds, then, Monsieur le Marquis, spare her fresh and useless trials; at least give back to her desolate old age the calm which it has lost.'

Gaston listened, with his head bent down.

'Can you tell me,' he slowly asked, 'what you mean by consolation? What is the language which, in your opinion, I ought to hold towards my grandmother, in order that she may derive consolation from it?'

Mariette perhaps felt that she had gone too far; but the firmness and integrity of her character made all evasions repugnant to her.

'It is impossible, Monsieur le Marquis that there should be the least need for me to enter into any explanations; and even if there were, it is not I who ought to be called to give them. It is not for me to know anything of the differences which may exist between you and your grandmother. All that I am aware of is, that Madame de Saissières is at present undergoing trials which are greater than she can bear. It was that which, inconsiderately perhaps, made me determined to speak to you last night, when—'

'Yes, I know—when you found yourself in the

presence of that man. But if—had it been possible for me to listen to you—I had replied that my grandmother's proud and irritable character and her domineering ways had rendered our intercourse so difficult that I no longer knew how to address her, would you then have refused to give me some advice; to tell me, for instance, in what respect, during the scene which took place yesterday, I especially wounded her proud and defiant heart? My grandmother must surely have spoken to you about me after I quitted her.'

'All that I know,' answered Mariette, in a serious tone, 'is that your grandmother loves you; and that if you were to give to her the deference and affection she considers to be her due, she would be happy.'

'Affection, do you say? I have some affection for her, perhaps, in spite of the tyranny—the word is not too strong—to which she has subjected me during so many years past. But as to *deference;* if it involves the being guilty of a weakness which would be near akin to villany; if, in order to sa t is f mother, I must renounce the dearest affections of my heart—'

'Allow me to withdraw, M. le Marquis. It is not from a poor girl like myself that you ought to ask advice respecting matters such as these. You will see, or you will not see, Madame de Saissières in accordance with what you may deem right. The only thing which I conjure you not to forget is that your grandmother is very old, alas! and that a renewal of the agitation from which she has lately suffered—I am sure of it from what I saw yesterday—may kill her.'

'I will depart, then, without going to her,' said Gaston, retreating. 'To deliver her from my presence is all I can do for her—tell her so. But of what good will that be? I beg to thank you, mademoiselle, for the care you have been so good as to give to my grandmother May I hope that you will continue to devote yourself to her? Your attention will become more necessary to her now than ever.'

'You alone can do anything for her, and yet it is you who are abandoning her!' exclaimed Mariette, almost in spite of herself.

'To leave her, never to see her again, is all I can do for her. You yourself must be aware of *that*.'

'I! What do you mean, M. le Marquis?'

'Did you not, just now, desire me at least to restore calm to her desolate old age?'

'Yes, if you will do no more.'

'Say rather, if I *cannot*, mademoiselle.'

Mariette was about to make a rejoinder, but she restrained herself. Gaston had seen the movement of her lips.

'Speak, I beg of you,' he said.

Just then the young girl thought only of the Marquise, and the despair which the prospect of the approaching departure of her grandson would cause her. Judging the hearts of others by her own, she felt as though it were the life of her old friend which was at stake at that moment.

'Take care, M. le Marquis,' she exclaimed, carried away by a momentary impetuosity; 'take care how you say, "I cannot," too hastily! You are about to quit your grandmother because it is, you tell me, impossible for you to satisfy her. If you had already made the endeavour without attaining success, that would be no reason for your not attempting it again. Are you quite certain that she is too exacting? And if she be, is it not for your sake, and because she loves you more perhaps than you imagine? Then think of her age, of the short space of time remaining to her in which to give you her blessing. Think, above all, what would be your despair if you were, one day, obliged to confess to yourself that you had shortened her life.'

Mariette paused, bewildered and astonished at her own boldness. The Marquis listened to her thoughtfully.

'All that may be quite true,' he murmured; 'but it is too late. I can no longer dispose of myself. Yes, it is too late.'

'I cannot bear to hear you speak in such a manner,' exclaimed Mariette, with a vehemence which confounded her even whilst she was yielding to it.

'It is never too late to do what is right. Come back to yourself, M. le Marquis; show that you are worthy of the name you bear. There are no faults which cannot be repaired, which cannot be redeemed, where the will is not wanting.'

Mariette spoke as though she had been in a dream; she was about to continue, when speech suddenly failed her. Seized with violent shivering and vertigo, she felt that the thread of her ideas was broken, a cloud enveloped her thoughts, and her knees refused to support her. She turned instinctively away, and regained the château with a tottering step. The Marquis, motionless and preoccupied, did not even perceive that she had left him.

The young girl reached the apartment of the Marquise without knowing how she got there. She felt as though she were walking on air; vague noises resounded in her ears; her eyes, covered with a mist, could no longer clearly distinguish the objects around her. She approached the bed where the Marquise was lying, and found that she had awoke; she tried to speak to her, but could not. She felt her limbs stiffening, her head was convulsively thrown back, and involuntarily uttering a cry, she fell her whole length upon the floor in a state of unconsciousness.

On the evening of that same day Mariette lay stiff and cold upon her bed, whilst the Curé and the Marquise, their eyes moist with tears, exchanged sorrowful glances as they stood on either side of her couch, entreating God to inspire them with a hope, in which the doctor who had been hastily summoned dared not indulge.

CHAPTER VII.

'QUICK, Johanna, quick! We shall never have finished. How slow you are! how very slow!'

And the good Curé became impatient. No, he was not impatient, but he was very much agitated, and Johanna was so confused she did not know what she was doing. She was busy putting into some poor little vases a few late-blowing flowers which were still blooming in the presbytery garden, and which were intended to give a festive appearance to Mariette's chamber. In fact, it was necessary that the whole of the presbytery should have a festal air. A good will had compensated an insufficiency of resources. For the last two days Johanna had been incessantly scouring and rubbing, and just then she had been making, in the most artistic manner possible, a series of the loveliest arabesques in the world, on the fine white sand which she had strewn over the pavement of the kitchen and passage. But what had been done in the presbytery itself was nothing in comparison with what had been effected outside, and with which neither the Curé nor Johanna had had anything whatever to do. The soil had been levelled with the greatest possible art, then beaten smoothly down with unparalleled vigour, and lastly covered with a layer of the finest sand. There was no longer the slightest risk of sinking into a puddle, even if all the windows of heaven should be opened, and the rain pour down in torrents. Moreover, on each side of the door a may-bush was proudly planted; but these bushes, proud as they looked, had simply been stolen out of the forest at a moment when the keeper was forgetting himself in the public-house at the corner of the village. I fancy that the Curé rather suspected it, though he tried his best to prevent himself from seeing the trees, otherwise it would have been his duty to administer a scolding. But scold whom? Well, that big fellow of a Joseph, who had made all these preparations out of his own head, without saying anything to any one. The Curé would not have been able to find it in his heart to scold just then, or address one harsh word to him; he was so happy. Besides, was it not right he should take into account Joseph's good intention? The Curé had his own ideas with regard to the subject of good intentions. He held that so far from hell, as the proverb says, being paved with them, they form a ladder, by means of which, however low may be the spot on which it is placed, we may climb at last to heaven. As good-for-nothing Joseph retained a lively remembrance of certain charities which had been bestowed on him by the Curé when he had fallen ill,

and was in great distress, abandoned by all the world
—for he had no relations, and no one in the village
cared for him—it is impossible he should not soon
understand that stolen fir-trees are never anything else
than stolen fir-trees, even when, through gratitude, they
are converted into may-bushes.

'I hear the carriage, Johanna,' exclaimed the
Curé. 'Johanna, have you finished?'

'Yes,' cried Johanna, placing another flower in the
last of the bouquets. 'There, I have done.'

They hastened together towards the porch; but
the Curé's soutane and Johanna's dress caught the
table, dragged off the blue-cloth cover embroidered
with yellow flowers—a new table-cover too, intended
to be a surprise!—and in a moment everything was on
the ground: table-cover, vases, flowers, and water;
and, alas, the vases were broken!

Johanna uttered a hollow groan, the Curé raised
his hands, and I imagine that he was tempted to
clench his fists; but he certainly did not do so: he
even restrained a rather sharp exclamation, through
which his vexation, his sorrow—the word is not too
strong—was about to find vent. He sighed—that
was all.

'Vanity of vanities!' he cried.

Then he hastened to the door.

A carriage had just stopped there; it was the
Marquis de Saissières'. A footman let down the steps,

and a young man jumped out and advanced to shake hands with the Curé. It was Gaston de Saissières. With manifest and great solicitude he then helped a young girl—who was no other than Mariette—to descend. Pallid, and scarcely convalescent, she fell into her uncle's arms. Then the Marquise got out of the carriage, and, leaning upon her grandson, entered the presbytery. When they had reached the parlour, of which Johanna, confused though she was, had yet retained sufficient presence of mind to open the door, they all sat down. The room contained precisely four comfortable chairs, which had just been newly stuffed. There was no other furniture, excepting a table covered with a small cloth, a cupboard of painted wood, and over the chimneypiece a copper crucifix, placed between two bouquets of artificial flowers standing in vases of alabaster. No one spoke; every one seemed agitated. Johanna, flattened against the door, twirled a corner of her apron between her fingers, and from time to time rubbed her eyes, as though she would like to have had a good cry.

'M. le Curé,' at length said the Marquise, in an affectionate tone, 'we restore our dear Mariette to you; but it is not without an effort that I yield her up. In my selfishness I should have liked to steal the child from you, if I had been able. I have done all I possibly could to keep her by my side; but it was mistaking her heart to imagine that I could separate her from you. I therefore gained nothing by my evil intentions. Mariette was determined to return to her home. Whatever may be the grief which her departure causes me—for I do not know what will become of me without her—I must confess that she has acted rightly. Thanks for having given to me, during the season of my sickness, this little angel-guardian, in whose train resignation and composure first arrived, and then something which even bears a resemblance to happiness. And you, dear and blessed child, what shall I say to you? How shall I thank you? You have been my consolation, my support, my pattern; you have taught me to know and to love—dare I add to practise?—the sweet and gentle virtues which in my folly I had thought were unworthy of great souls. You have shown me the value and the grandeur of submission to the will of God. And God, in His goodness, as soon as He saw that I was submissive, gave back to me the grandson whom I wept. It is to you, my child, that I owe this supreme favour, because it is through you I have learnt how to merit it.'

Mariette had in vain attempted to interrupt the Marquise. Failing to do so, she bent her head, as though all these eulogiums wounded her.

'Madame,' answered the Curé, 'if my niece has been able to soften your trials by her presence I am repaid, and more than repaid, for the effort which it cost me to separate myself, even though it was only temporarily, from my child; and whatever it might have cost me I should have allowed her to remain with you still, if she herself had not been of opinion that her services were no longer necessary.'

'Her *services!*' exclaimed Madame de Saissières; 'what a word to use! It is not services, but affection, which I desire to receive from her. Why cannot she, after having shared in my sorrow, partake in our joys? after having associated herself in our trials to such an extent as to injure her health, and even her life, why will she not allow us to enable her to enjoy some tranquil happy days in the dwelling where she has caused peace and joy once more to enter? It is doubtless you, M. le Curé, who will not give your permission.'

'Pardon me, madame,' said the young girl, in a firm but gentle tone, 'I have not even consulted my uncle. He would, perhaps, have advised me to yield to the wishes you have been so kind as to express that I should remain with you. I leave you, madame, because my place is here, and nowhere else. If I have rendered you some slight services, I thank God for enabling me to do so. As to the kindness you have shown me, I shall never forget it.'

Mariette spoke with visible effort. The Marquise pressed her hand without making any answer, and withdrew immediately with her grandson.

When the carriage, which had brought them to the house, had gone out of sight, there was an explosion of joy on the part of the Curé and of Johanna. They were never tired of telling Mariette how delighted they were to see her again, or how they had missed her, and they thanked her a hundred times for having come back to them. The young girl did her best to respond to their demonstrations of affection; but she was still weak, and every now and then it seemed as though her breath would fail her. Leaning on the arm of her uncle, she slowly paced through the garden, showed an interest in some changes which had been made, and admired Johanna's pears and even her cabbages. They continued their walk until the Curé, remarking how pale his niece had become, fancied that she was tired, and took her back to the house.

'Alas,' said he, opening the door of her room, 'see what a misfortune has happened! Your vases are broken! It is Johanna and I who are in fault.'

They discovered, however, that only one was broken, and so the flowers were all placed in the other. When Mariette at last found herself alone in her little chamber, she carefully closed the door, and sitting down, cast a long and melancholy glance around her, weeping bitterly the while. Then she tried to pray, but it was only her lips which spoke to God, and not her heart and her soul. Hearing

Johanna knocking gently at the door, she dried her eyes, and went to her uncle, who was in the parlour.

'Have you taken a little rest?' he inquired, as soon as he saw her. 'I wager you have not, you are still so pale.'

'I do not feel tired,' was Mariette's reply, whilst her face was already resuming its placid look.

'Not tired, child! Why did you not come down to me at once, then? What have you been doing up-stairs?'

'I have been praying a little, uncle, if you really wish to know.'

'Sleep is a good thing, but prayer is a better, my darling. You have done well. I also have been praying. I wanted to thank God for having brought us together once more. Do you know that during your illness there was a moment when I could not help asking myself if He was not about to take you to Himself. For the first time in my life I had not courage to say, "Thy will be done." The words would not come. My mouth refused to utter them, or, at any rate, my heart would not ratify them.'

Mariette replied by a glance of affection. Some time afterwards she asked her uncle whether he thought of going on the following day to the château.

'No; what have I got to do there now that you are no longer there?'

'Why do you speak in that way, uncle? Suppose Madame de Saissières wanted you?'

'In that case I shall, as always, be at her service. But you know quite well that there is no likelihood of anything of the kind happening.'

'And how should I know it?'

'Through the Marquise, who must certainly have told you herself.'

'She never said anything, excepting that she was happy, and that her grandson—'.

'That her grandson was everything she could wish.'

'It is quite true. And now as peace has been once more restored to the château, and the worthless visitors who had invaded its precincts have taken their departure, I have nothing more to do there. Madame de Saissières does not know yet, nor will she ever know, how much cause she has to bless you, Mariette.'

'What do you mean?' asked the young girl, whilst her cheeks were suffused with a slight flush.

'Was it not through you that I was able to get at a knowledge of a portion, at any rate, of the truth, and that I succeeded in discovering the secret of the inexplicable power which was being exercised over the young Marquis? Ah, if he had but been open with me a little sooner, how much sorrow he might have spared us all! How fearful is the power which pride exercises over us, and which, in order to spare us the confession of our faults, causes us to commit so many others! I shall never forget the scene I had with the Marquis when, seeing that he would not speak, I said all at once, "I know everything; my niece has told me."'

'What, uncle?' exclaimed Mariette impetuously; 'did you repeat to M. de Saissières all that the stranger said to me?'

'I only told him what it was right I should tell him, my child. And I should not have mentioned your name, excepting that it was necessary for me to explain how I had come upon the traces of this wretched secret. There was no mention made of you afterwards. It was from the person to whom you refer that I heard the rest.'

'How were you able to hide it all from the Marquise?'

'I had no difficulty in doing so, for this time I had nothing more to do than to purchase, not Gaston's departure, but his liberty. I told Madame de Saissières so, begging her at the same time not to ask me for any other explanations. She had confidence in me, and authorised me to act as I might deem right, furnishing me, at the same time, with means whereby to bring the affair to a conclusion.'

'And,' said Mariette hesitatingly, 'if I were to ask you to give me some explanations, should I be doing wrong?'

'You would certainly do much better not to ask me for any.'

'Then I will not, but it was not an indiscreet curiosity which induced me to wish for some explanation.'

'No, I am sure of that. I perfectly understand your affection for the Marquise, and your desire to be set perfectly at ease in regard to her future. Let it be sufficient for you to know that we have been able, by means of a sum of money, to deliver the young Marquis from the threats which the person, whom you saw that night at the château, was holding over his head, and that peace has been established between the grandson and grandmother. Warned by the severe lesson she has had to learn, the Marquise no longer treats the young man as a child whom she is holding in leading-strings; and on his side, the Marquis now sees how much consideration is due towards the misfortunes and age of his grandmother; so that everything is going on as well as possible.'

'These are indeed joyful tidings, uncle. How glad I should be if I could persuade myself that I had in any degree contributed, as you say, to bring about so unexpected a change! But—but it seems to me that a special cause of disagreement existed between Madame de Saissières and her grandson.'

'O, yes—certain matrimonial projects—'

'Well, uncle?'

'Well, my child, all *that* is at an end.'

Mariette was silent for a few moments; then she said, in rather a hesitating manner,

'What could the unhappy young man have possibly done that he should have been at the mercy of—of the stranger whom I saw at the château?'

'Do you not think, child,' said her uncle, 'that we are talking a little too much about other people's affairs? We ought not to occupy ourselves with them, excepting in so far as we may have some service to render, some good to effect. There is nothing of the kind in question at the present moment. Let us, then, quit the subject.'

The day passed tranquilly and even gaily, at least as far as regarded the Curé and Johanna. Mariette was still too weak, doubtless, to be able to be very demonstrative. She did all in her power, however, to show how happy she was to find herself once more with those who loved her so dearly. But in order to laugh, a long breath is required, otherwise a sigh is apt involuntarily to escape us from time to time.

The next day Madame de Saissières came with her grandson to inquire after her young friend, and to attempt to persuade her to go very soon to the château and spend a few hours there. Alleging her want of strength, Mariette refused. During the following fortnight, the Marquise renewed her visits, allowing, however, by degrees a longer space to pass between them. By little and little, the Curé's niece resumed her habitual manner of life, but she did not recover the youthful freshness or the sweet animation which had formerly rendered her so charming. Her uncle, who had attentively observed her, said to her one day,

'Now, my child, what is the matter with you? you are either ill or out of spirits. If you are ill, what is it you are suffering from? If you are out of spirits, what is the cause?'

'I am neither out of spirits nor ill,' said Mariette, starting.

'I do not like that kind of answer,' replied her uncle, shaking his head; 'it is not sincere. Since you will not confess the truth, I will tell you myself what I fancy I see. Ill you are not; no! You only need a little blood in your cheeks and a little strength. All that would soon come back if your heart were at rest. It is not there that the evil is to be sought. You do not like being here; I understand that. You had by slow degrees accustomed yourself to our simple manner of life; but the time you have spent at the château has caused you to lose the fruits of a long endeavour. There you found the luxury and the kind of life which reminded you of the past. The Curé's house is ugly and melancholy; I understand that. Poverty does not suit all kinds of characters; you feel a little stifled here; this contracted and limited existence, monotonous as it is, produces upon you the impression of a narrow sunken road, along which you have to walk always straight on, without seeing anything, after having freely traversed flowery meadows. I repeat that I understand it all. When one feels that one is born for a château, it is hard to find oneself condemned to a presbytery. It is that, is it not? Remember that you owe it to me to speak the truth.'

'Absolutely, as though I were in your confessional, uncle,' said Mariette, smiling, 'I will tell you the truth, and you will see—that you do not in the least understand me! It is entirely of my own free will and with gladness of heart that I have come back. I might have prolonged my sojourn at the château. I did not do so, because I desired, as soon as possible, to resume at your side my narrow straitened life, as you call it, but a life full of sweetness and of repose; the only life which henceforth it will be possible for me to love. Did you not listen, only a few days ago, to the persuasions the Marquise addressed to me, in order to induce me to visit the château; and did you not hear my refusal? Believe me, my dear uncle, it is here, it is beside you, that I wish to live and find peace.'

'You are not happy, however?'

'I am as happy as I can be.'

'It seems to me that is hardly—'

'What! is it your little Mariette who is obliged

to remind her uncle, her Curé, that we did not come into this world in order to be happy?'

'You are making a mock at me, I fancy, my child,' said the Curé, smiling, and sighing at the same time. 'But you are not going to escape in that way. You *ought* to be happy. You have a right to the happiness promised in this world to those who perform their duty. I mean the only true happiness—that which springs from a quiet conscience, from a soul which trusts in God, and from a heart filled with love towards Him.'

'And, if you please, uncle, who told you that I do not possess the happiness you describe? You speak as if I had neither a tranquil conscience, nor confidence in God, nor any love for Him. But it is quite a mistake! What is it you think of me? Will you not, one of these days, be finding out that I am a great criminal?'

'You make me say the most horrible things, my child, in order that you may not be obliged to give me an answer. But in one word, which is as good as a hundred, you are melancholy and out of spirits; you no longer have any of the animation which I used to delight to see in you—that spontaneous cheerfulness which proves that we are grateful to God for the blessings which He bestows upon even the most humble life. What is the matter?'

'To ask me such a question,' said Mariette sorrowfully, 'is to address to me a bitter reproach. It is as much as to say that I am ungrateful towards God and towards you. Is it possible that it could be so? Do not tell me that I am sad; how could I be? and why? If I am no longer what I ought to be to you, I am unconscious of it—I will watch over myself. I am still, perhaps, rather unwell. Dear uncle, I beg you to have patience; you will soon see me become once more all that you could wish. Yes, I will promise to be cheerful.'

But even whilst she was promising to be cheerful, Mariette seemed as though she were ready to weep, and, indeed, a few tears flowed down her cheeks.

'We will not say another word about it,' cried the Curé, with affectionate earnestness. 'I will not have you putting a restraint on yourself; your nerves have not yet recovered their tone. It is all clear enough. The emotions, the fright, the illness you have undergone—you must have time to recover from it all. I heartily wish you could have a few simple and innocent pleasures. We lead too austere a life for a girl of your age; I am very tiresome, and so is Johanna. We must find—'

'What are you talking about, uncle?' exclaimed Mariette, laughing heartily this time at the simplicity with which the good Curé declared that he was 'very tiresome.'

'Yes, indeed, I am very tiresome, and Johanna is

not very amusing. Is it not true, Johanna?' he cried, as he saw the old servant enter the room.

'What do you say, M. le Curé?' asked the old woman, who was rather hard of hearing.

'I said,' replied the Curé, 'that we were too old for Mariette—you and me; that of course we must weary her; that she has just been ill; that she needs something to amuse her a little. But an idea has just come into my head. You have a cousin who is a nun, have you not, Johanna?'

'Yes, M. le Curé,' said Johanna, drawing herself up; 'and not only that, but she is superior of the convent of—'

'Uncle,' interrupted Mariette, 'I declare, with all the respect which is due to you, that your idea is perfectly void of common sense, and I do not even want to know what it is. As for you, Johanna, instead of speaking to us about your cousin who is a superior, you will be better employed in going to the poultry-yard and seeing after your hens. Just listen to the noise they are making! A cat—a weasel perhaps.'

'Holy Virgin! there really must be something,' cried Johanna, listening with all her might. 'They never cackle as loudly as that for nothing.'

And she quitted the room hastily.

'Let us also go and see why the hens are cackling in that way,' exclaimed Mariette, dragging her uncle after her.

From that day, whether it was owing to an effort of the will or to a real change in her feelings, the young girl was more cheerful. But her health became a subject of serious anxiety to her uncle. Her appetite failed her more and more, and her strength also. The Curé confided his uneasiness to Johanna, who understood hens better than sick people, and so she contented herself with saying that Mariette ought to take a raw egg every morning to strengthen her digestion. At last the Curé consulted the doctor who attended at the château. After having paid Mariette a visit he left her, saying that she required to be 'tonified.'

'To be tonified,' said the Curé sadly; 'there is nothing I desire more than that she should be strengthened. But how is that to be managed?'

'We can have recourse to a hundred different kinds of tonics, not one of which is worth a pinch of snuff, my dear Curé. There is, in fact, but one means whereby to recover lost strength — namely, to eat, drink, and sleep.'

'In one word, to be in good health; is not that it?'

'Yes; you are right.'

'Well, I did not need you to help me to make such a discovery as that.'

The Curé went to the château to impart his anxiety to the Marquise, whom he had not seen for some time, and to ask her advice. She listened with interest, and then said,

'Your dear little Mariette is *ennuyée;* that is what is the matter with her. The child was not brought up for the kind of life which she leads in your house. She is trying to do more than she can. Without confessing it to herself, she feels as though she could not breathe in your little presbytery, and if you do not take care she will die.'

'Ah, madame!' exclaimed the Curé, starting, 'what good is thére in telling me to take care, if I cannot find any remedy, and if no one will give me any?'

'I will do so, then. She must be amused.'

'Very well; but nothing does amuse her. You are like your doctor, who told me that she must be "tonified."'

'Patience, Curé! You will find in me, not only the doctor who will prescribe the medicine, but the druggist who will make it up, and the sick nurse who will administer it. Give me Mariette for a short time, and I will restore her to you more blooming and gay than ever.'

'And for the future utterly incapable, of course, of returning to the modest and simple way of life which it is her lot to lead. No, Madame la Marquise, that prescription cannot possibly be administered. The remedy is worse than the disease.'

'M. le Curé,' said the Marquise, who did not like to be interrupted, 'you are taking a great responsibility upon yourself.'

'I fancy you want to make an appeal to my conscience,' said the Curé, with a feeble smile; 'but in what does the responsibility consist when one only endeavours to do one's duty?'

'It is true. I was wrong to address you in such a manner. Big Jean, in person, would not have spoken otherwise to his Curé. But the fact is that I love little Mariette dearly, and that I want to do her good. You can certainly confess her, but I know better than you do what young girls require. Once more I beg you to let me have her for a few months. You will not? Quite decided? Well, after all, you are perhaps right. I have something else, then, to propose. Will you allow me to make her a little present? You are going to ask me what present, I suppose? You must have sufficient confidence in me to allow me *carte blanche* in the matter. As to the rest, if my present does not please you, or should it be unsuitable for your niece, you can refuse it, and there will be an end of it.'

The Curé took his departure, without feeling much confidence that the present the Marquise intended to make would restore health to Mariette and remove his anxiety.

CHAPTER VIII.

THE next day, just as the Curé and his niece were finishing their modest dinner, which Mariette had hardly touched, the sound of horses' footsteps was heard approaching the presbytery. A groom made his appearance on horseback at the porch, leading by the bridle a beautiful and spirited mare, on whose back was a lady's saddle. Johanna went to the door, and after a few words had passed between her and the man, she came into the room in a state of agitation, and handed to Mariette a letter and parcel which had been sent her by the Marquise. The letter, which contained a few lines only, written in a firm hand, was as follows:

'My Child,—You have done me a great deal of good, and you must allow me to do you a little in return. Air and exercise are necessary for you. Mount the little mare which I am sending you, and which I think must resemble the one your father once gave you, judging by what you have told me. It is yours. It will, however, remain at the château; but every day, at your hour for taking exercise, it will be at your door with the groom, whom I present to you as your servant, and who is as safe as old Lambert himself. Here, too, is a riding-habit. Pardon me for having sent you one which I have myself worn; I thought that most likely you had not anything of the kind yourself now. This one is old-fashioned. I remember it was said I looked beautiful when I had it on. Vanity of vanities! I beautiful! You, my darling, you are charming and you are loved—you know how much. But why, little hermit, why will you no longer come and see your very affectionate old friend, MARQUISE DE SAISSIÈRES?'

Dumb with surprise, the young girl passed the letter over to her uncle, who shook his head whilst reading it.

'Well, uncle dear?'

'Well, child?'

'You do not say anything!'

'No, certainly. I am waiting for you to speak.'

'What do you wish me to say?'

'And what do you wish *me*?'

'You? That you should tell me what I ought to do, and what answer I ought to send.'

'It is for you to settle that.'

'For me to decide?—me! But, uncle, it is impossible. It is you alone who know what all this means. You saw the Marquise yesterday; of course she spoke to you about it.'

'She told me that she wanted to make you a present—nothing more.'

'And you consented? You think that I ought—that I can—'

'I do not think anything. I tell you that you are free to do what you like.'

The pretty mare, as though she guessed that she was the subject of conversation, was noisily prancing at the door. Mariette went to the window to look at her. She was so spirited, so full of life, so graceful. Without being aware of it, the young girl's eyes danced with pleasure. The Curé observed her in silence. As she stood lost in thought, which brought a fugitive flush to her sunken cheek, he said to her,

'I will only give you one solitary piece of advice. It is that you should not make the groom uselessly wait. Whatever it may be that you decide upon, do it at once.'

'I am going to write to Madame de Saissières and refuse her present,' said Mariette.

And she began to write. Nothing in the expression of her face would have led any one to imagine that she was making at that moment a great effort—or rather, a sacrifice. But that day she was even more pallid than usual. Her uncle was struck by it. He recalled to mind what the Marquise had said to him: 'She will die of it;' and he felt overwhelmed.

'Come,' said he, 'let us see. Suppose you were

to try the mare? Without accepting it as a present, you might sometimes ride the little beast, which, I am sure, is not used by any one at the château, and it will do you good.'

Mariette, holding up her pen, gazed at her uncle with a questioning expression.

'Confess,' he went on, 'that it would give you great pleasure to ride.'

Wise Mariette would have liked to say, No; but truth-telling Mariette was obliged to confess that she believed she should still find a little pleasure in the exercise.

'Well,' replied the Curé, with a sigh, 'leave your letter there; I will reply to the Marquise. I will tell her it is not possible you should have a horse of your own; but that if she will be good enough to lend you the little mare every now and then, I shall be happy to allow you to ride now and then, for the sake of your health.'

Mariette hesitated and seemed half overcome. But encouraged and pressed by her uncle, she recovered herself immediately. The Marquise's old riding-habit would have been too large for her; she therefore only put on the skirt over her little cotton dress, and in a moment she had arranged for herself a headdress out of a garden-hat, the brim of which she turned up under a veil. The Curé was at once happy and uneasy at seeing her make these preparations with an animation such as she had not shown for a long time past.

'If I knew you less well,' he said, shaking his head, 'I should be afraid that you were going to resume your liking for vanities.'

'Do you think there is the least fear of it?' asked Mariette, with sudden sadness.

'No, my child. Go!'

Helped by the groom, and scarcely touching with her foot the knee which he bent, the young girl vaulted into her saddle; then she set off, saying to her uncle, who was looking at her, as he stood on the threshold,

'I shall not be long away.'

He went back into the house, full of anxiety.

'Have I done wrong?' he asked himself. 'It is a trial—'

Johanna, her eyes wide open, her hands clasped, looked at the pair as they rode away, and exclaimed,

'Jesus, Maria! How she keeps her seat!'

And, lounging by the roadside, big Joseph, curious, like all good-for-nothing fellows are, also looked at them; and although it was not easy for him to be astonished, he was so completely and suddenly taken by surprise that he ceased from his eternal whistling.

As soon as they had left the village behind them, Mariette gave the reins to her impatient steed and rode towards the forest. Restored thus suddenly to what had formerly been one of her greatest pleasures, she gave herself up to it like the child she still was, spite of all her common sense. She had been galloping for some time along shady avenues, when the mare became suddenly excited by hearing the gallop of an animal in her rear. Fancying that it was the groom who was attempting to overtake her, in order, perhaps, to warn her that it was time for him to return to the château, she did her best to master her steed and wheel it round. It was not the groom, however, but another cavalier, who was approaching her at a hasty gallop. He soon reached her, and putting his horse beside Mariette's, as well as accommodating his pace to hers, he bowed and smiled. It was the Marquis Gaston de Saissières.

'How fast you are going, mademoiselle!' he said gaily. 'I fancied I should never overtake you. Are we going to continue at the same pace for any length of time?'

Mariette had so little anticipated such a meeting that at first she was utterly at a loss for an answer, and contented herself with merely bowing in reply. She tried to bring the mare to a walk, but she refused, and began to prance.

'Why do you want to prevent the small creature from galloping, when it has such a longing to do so?' asked Gaston. 'Shall we go on a little longer at the same pace? What do you say?'

'I think I have galloped long enough,' said Mariette, with a tinge of embarrassment; 'I am rather tired.'

Then there took place between her mare and herself a very animated struggle, which the young man watched with interest, ready to interfere if it were necessary. Feeling that she was in danger of being thrown, Mariette gave all her attention to her steed, and succeeded in mastering it.

'My sincere compliments, mademoiselle,' said Gaston, again taking up his post beside her. 'Foolish Dinah knows there is nothing for it but submission. You manage her admirably. I was almost uneasy at first, when I found that my grandmother had sent you the mare, well broken in though she be, but still a little too spirited, perhaps. I was reassured, however, when I was told that you rode to perfection; and I now see, in fact, that there is no reason to fear for you. You are very kind, mademoiselle, to have consented to accept this little present from my grandmother. If you had refused, it would have pained her greatly.'

'Madame la Marquise is only too good,' murmured Mariette, paralysed by a strange and insurmountable embarrassment. 'But I ought not—I believe—I think —that my uncle—'

'Your uncle will, of course, have told you that you cannot refuse,' said Gaston, without appearing to remark the young girl's agitation. 'It is all so very simple: my grandmother feels that she can never be grateful enough for all the good you have done her. I must even be allowed to add, that you have done *us*.'

Mariette made no reply. He continued:

'How sad it cannot but be for us to think that your health has suffered from the fatigue and agitation you underwent during your sojourn at the château! I should be so happy, mademoiselle, if you could assure me that you have ceased to suffer from the effects of it.'

'I am perfectly well,' Mariette hastily replied. 'It would distress me if Madame de Saissières were to imagine that it was owing, as you say, monsieur, to the fatigue, the—'

She could not finish her sentence.

'My grandmother does not know all,' said Gaston. 'She has been allowed to remain in ignorance of what took place during the night on which, seeing her so ill, you endeavoured to come and find me. I owe you my thanks, mademoiselle, for the delicacy you have shown in concealing all these details from her. Neither did you say anything to her of the fright you experienced one evening when you went into my father's room.'

Mariette trembled. The remembrance of that inexplicable occurrence had often presented itself to her. How was it possible Gaston should know anything about it? Reading a question in the glance which involuntarily she gave him—

'It was I who was in the room,' said the young Marquis. 'When I felt sad and out of heart I used sometimes to go there and think of the father whom I have never known, and from whom, I believe, I should have met with more indulgence than I have received from my grandmother. Startled by the sound of your footsteps, imagining that I was about to see my grandmother appear, and knowing that had she found me she would have been certain to say that I had gone there actuated by some evil intention, I instinctively extinguished my candle, and retired into the alcove. Afterwards, when you also directed your steps towards it, I felt as though I were in so absurd a position, and, to say the truth, in so humiliating a one, that I blew out your candle too, intending to make my escape in the darkness. It was all very ridiculous on my part, I confess. Losing your way, you came towards the bed; your hand touched mine as it lay on the coverlid. Your scream, and the noise you made in falling, showed me how awkward I had been.'

Mariette, recalling to mind that she had found herself in the picture-gallery without being able to explain how she had got there, and feeling sure that it must have doubtless been Gaston who had carried her thither, remained silent and overwhelmed with confusion.

'I am delighted,' continued Gaston, 'to have had an opportunity of making an explanation to you respecting what happened in that gloomy chamber. You must have found it very unpleasant not to be able to understand it.'

'Yes,' murmured Mariette; but at the same time she could not help asking herself whether, after all, she would not have preferred to have been told that she had touched the hand of the deceased Marquis, than to have discovered that she had been carried in the arms of his son.

Gaston continued:

'During several succeeding days I reproached myself for all the harm I had done you, and longed to speak to you, but it was difficult, almost impossible, to see you alone; and besides, to tell you the truth, I was very unhappy just then, absorbed by heavy anxieties, and at last I ceased to dwell on what had occurred. It comes back to me now that, thanks to you, I have once more found peace. Far, indeed, was I from thinking that you were destined to render such a service to me when I suddenly saw you that first evening in the drawing-room where I was lying asleep. Do you remember it? You had brought your uncle his shoes. I was lying upon a sofa. What an odd meeting it was!'

Gaston laughed heartily, but it was a laugh exempt from the slightest tinge of ridicule. Mariette, however, felt herself flush at the recollection of the pair of shoes.

'I was saying,' went on the young man, with animation, 'that I was very far from suspecting just then that you were destined to be the instrument of my deliverance; and yet you were, mademoiselle—you and your excellent uncle, the very Curé whom I could not endure, and whom I sent sometimes—dare I venture to tell you?—to the devil, to whom I was going as fast as I could myself. You have been my two saviours.'

Mariette stopped her mare, and then gently wheeled her round.

'It seems that we are to take another road,' said the Marquis. 'Where are we going now?'

'I am returning to the presbytery,' said Mariette, with a little hesitation. 'I am tired.'

'That is a pity! It is delightful in the forest. However, you must not try your strength too much just at first. You must get gradually accustomed to horse-exercise. The habit will come back to you very quickly. Then I will show you some very interesting rides in the neighbourhood. I am well acquainted with them, as I have taken them a hundred times during my hours of impatience and ennui, when I was already meditating about liberating myself by flight from my grandmother's dominion. Would to God,' he added, with a sigh, 'that that dominion had been less severe, or that I had been more docile! What sorrow I should have spared numbers of people! But

K

we will not speak about that, will we? since they are things which are passed away for ever. Meanwhile, until you are able to take long rides, we will go some pretty short ones, which will not fatigue you. You will consent, will you not? Do not say no! I will beg your uncle and my grandmother to make you.'

Mariette murmured a few words of thanks.

'Do not say "thank you," I beg. It is pure selfishness on my part. I shall be delighted to ride with you. There is no one whose society I now prefer to yours. That sounds strange, does it not? But it is because there is something about you which inspires sympathy, and, I may add, a kind of affection.'

Noticing the serious expression of Mariette's face,

'Pardon,' said he; 'you think perhaps that I am putting myself too much at my ease with you. But why should I not offer you, after all, an affection which is almost fraternal? Do not answer me. It was foolish of me to speak to you in that way. Let us talk of something else.'

And without any prelude he immediately began to speak of the Curé—of the good he did; of the affection and respect with which he inspired every one with whom he came in contact; and thus talking, he brought back the young girl to the presbytery. After helping her to dismount from her horse, he bowed to her affectionately, and then said, 'Until to-morrow, is not it?' As Mariette did not reply, he passed from an interrogative to an affirmative tone.

'Until to-morrow, then, mademoiselle,' he repeated, lifting his hat.

So saying he got into his saddle and set off, followed in the distance by the groom, who led Mariette's horse.

The young girl reached her room without having met any one. The Curé and Johanna were in the garden. She took off her long skirt and her improvised headdress; then looking at herself in her little mirror, which was hardly bigger than her hand,

'Just so,' said she. 'There is the Curé's niece. Nothing more. Let us never forget it, even if it be for but one moment.'

Then she went down-stairs, and joined her uncle in the garden.

'Well,' said he, looking at her, 'and the Marquise's present? How did you like it?'

'First of all,' answered Mariette, leaning affectionately on her uncle's arm, 'I thought it an excellent and charming animal.'

'I have no doubt it is; and afterwards?'

'That I had mounted it to-day for the first and last time; and that if you will be so kind, uncle, as to accompany me, we will go to-morrow and thank the Marquise for her kind intentions, and tell her that it is impossible for me to take advantage of them.'

'Really, my child! and why?'

'Because of several reasons, uncle.'

'What are they?'

'Will you oblige me to tell you?'

'Certainly I will not oblige you, if you prefer to keep them to yourself.'

'To tell the truth, I do prefer.'

'We will not say anything more about the matter, then, my child. Your reasons cannot be anything but good and praiseworthy. So we shall not see you again in a riding-habit?'

'No, never.'

'Well, so much the better. I did not wish to say anything to you before, because it was right to leave you to your own feelings, in which I always have confidence; but my heart was heavy when I saw you going off in that way. I no longer recognised my dear and humble little Mariette in that long skirt.'

'Which I ought never to have put on,' said the poor girl, sincerely ashamed. 'O uncle, how good you are not to have addressed one single word of reproach to me! Was I not mad, when I allowed myself to be tempted for a moment by a horse? I could laugh at myself if I had courage to do so. I think that I can at least promise that you will never again see me fall into such forgetfulness of the past, of the present—and of myself.'

The Curé, without saying another word, pressed

her hand with emotion. During the evening Mariette was calm, cheerful even. She told her uncle how she had seen M. de Saissières in the forest, and that he had accompanied her, and had afterwards taken her back to the presbytery.

CHAPTER IX.

The following day the Curé and his niece went very early to the château.

'Ah,' cried the Marquise, as soon as she saw Mariette, 'I already see by the tinge of colour which has come back to your cheeks the good effects of my remedy. Well, my dear Curé, and what do you say? Will you not take me another time for your confidante and your doctor?'

Great was her surprise when she found that they refused to accept her present.

'The Curé has something to do with it,' she exclaimed, shaking her finger. 'It is your uncle's doing! But, my dear little one, I am not going to be as submissive as you, not I, and I shall rebel. The mare is yours. You took possession of it yesterday in a very brilliant manner, from what Gaston, who understands these matters well, tells me; and spite of all the curés and uncles in the world, it shall be yours always. It is very fine to-day, and the mare shall be sent for you at the same hour as yesterday.'

It was not without difficulty that Mariette succeeded in making her understand that the decision at which she had arrived was irrevocable and entirely spontaneous, and that the Curé had had nothing to do with it.

'But, at any rate, you will give me a good reason; I will not ask for more than one,' exclaimed the Marquise, who was beginning to get impatient.

At that moment her grandson entered the boudoir, and she told him in two words what had passed. Gaston turned round, and looked at Mariette with astonishment. The young girl, without allowing him time to reflect, or to question her, rose to take leave.

'Dear child,' the Marquise exclaimed, with vivacity, 'do you know I am beginning to think that you are a little obstinate? It is a grievous fault; and I, who have all along been imagining you perfect—shall I be obliged to make some deduction? What a deception it has been! And there is that uncle of yours standing there and keeping silence, instead of putting himself on our side, and helping us to make our little hard-hearted creature yield! Come, Gaston—you who yesterday saw her managing her steed so beautifully, so it seems—tell us if you think our pretty mare deserves such a repulse.'

Gaston doubtless saw, from the expression of her face, that his interference would displease the young girl, for he contented himself with saying that, whilst sharing in his grandmother's disappointment, he would take care not to hazard an attempt in which she had failed to succeed.

The Curé and his niece then took their departure, followed by the reproaches of the Marquise, and declining her invitation to dinner. When they had got outside the château,

'You do not regret,' asked the Curé, 'and you are sure that you will not regret, the mare?'

'Quite sure.'

'Yes, but these rides would have done you good; you would have been able to go out every day, and in that way we should have "tonified" you, as the doctor says. Instead of which, by continuing to live like a recluse, and never going beyond your little garden— Are you well aware, my child, that it is a positive duty for you to—'

'Stop, uncle; do not prescribe for me, as a duty, a thing which I would rather do from pleasure. You wish that I should walk? Well, then, I will take a walk every day with you.'

'Really?'

'Yes. Yesterday evening I felt quite ashamed at finding that the pleasure of mounting on horseback had all at once given me strength to do what you have in vain asked me to attempt for a long time past. I am sure you must yourself have made the same reflection. Will you forgive me?'

'Forgive you!' exclaimed the Curé—'forgive you!

But what is there which a little creature of the good God, such as you are, could possibly do to need pardon? The Marquise is a nice sort of person to have fancied that she has discovered you are not perfect! Ah, but what is it I am saying? It is very wrong; I am failing entirely in my duty by speaking to you after such a fashion as this. None of us here below are perfect. If any one were to believe himself perfect he would fall into the sin of pride, which is the most terrible sin of all, Mariette. Yes, my child, you are not devoid of faults.'

'I know it but too well.'

'You do things which require forgiveness.'

'I feel it more than you have any idea of, uncle,' she said sorrowfully.

'Yes, you ought to feel it—it is quite right you should. But, Mariette, you must never—do you hear?— ask pardon from your uncle. God, who knows everything, knows of course what your faults are. As for me, I do not see them; and far from thinking I have anything to forgive in you, I feel as though, on the contrary—well, it seems that I am beginning again, after all, to pay you compliments! We will not say anything more about the matter. What is it I was saying? Ah, yes; when shall we begin our walks?'

'To-day—this minute, uncle, if you like.'

'But are you not too tired? Yes, I see you are.'

'No, I would rather not go in at once. Let us

walk a little while. I will only ask you to let me lean on your arm.'

So they continued their ramble. The Curé was gay and talkative, doing everything in his power to amuse his niece, and to prove to her, so he said, 'that he was as good as a horse.' And she forced herself to smile, by way of responding to his amiability. At the turning of a road they suddenly found themselves in presence of the Marquis de Saissières.

'Pardon me for having disturbed you in your walk,' he said, advancing towards them. 'You had hardly left us, M. le Curé, when my grandmother recollected that she had something to say to you. Seeing that you had gone in this direction, and knowing that I could overtake you by making my way along a cross-road, I charged myself with her commission. But do not let me keep you standing. I will walk on with you, and tell you what it is the Marquise wishes me to say to you.'

It was about some miserably poor parishioners of the Curé's, who, after having for a long time past received help from the Marquise, had been accused of certain thefts; but representations being made to the Marquise, she had determined, prompt as she always was in her resolutions, to refuse henceforth to aid them in any way whatever. The Curé at once protested with some heat against her decision, and told the young Marquis that it would be most unjust to accept such accusations without having first listened to what the accused had to say for themselves.

'I know it,' said Gaston; 'but you are acquainted with my grandmother. The reports which have reached her, and which have so irritated her against these poor creatures, have been spread by people in whom she has every confidence. I do not see that there is any one, except yourself, M. le Curé, who has the least chance of inducing her to reconsider her determination.'

'I will make the attempt,' said the Curé. 'It is my duty to do so. First of all, however, I will go and question the culprits.'

'That will be best. I might help you in your inquiry, since I know exactly in what the accusations consist. Guilty or not, these people must live. If you do not succeed in softening my grandmother, I will make an arrangement with you, if you will kindly allow me, which will prevent them from feeling themselves completely abandoned.'

'Thank you in their name.'

'Will you go and see them to-day? Shall we continue our walk in that direction?'

'No,' said the Curé, fearing lest Mariette might be fatigued. 'I will go to-morrow.'

The subject exhausted, the Marquis did not, nevertheless, take his leave. He continued to walk beside Mariette and the Curé, speaking the while on indifferent subjects. He had travelled a little, had read a little, had seen the world a little, he knew a little about everything, and conversed agreeably. The Curé listened with interest. Mariette, annoyed at first by his presence, ended by taking some pleasure in hearing him talk. His perfect courtesy and the grace of his manners added to the charm of his language, which was always simple, but marked at the same time by a certain originality of thought and expression. The ramble was prolonged without any one making an objection. The Curé at last put an end to it, by declaring, after having consulted his watch, that they had been walking for a whole hour, and that it was long enough—too long, perhaps—for Mariette's strength to support, consequently they must return to the house. M. de Saissières quitted them at once.

'That young man is worth more than I imagined, said the Curé, looking at him as he pursued his way to the château. 'I begin to think that the cure is complete. He has a good deal of right feeling. You heard what he said to me about those poor people? I half wish that his grandmother would continue to remain implacable, and would thus give him the opportunity of performing a good work. One never does only a little good to others, dear Mariette, without doing a great deal to oneself. That is one of the marvellous effects of charity. But I am afraid that

I talked too long with the Marquis; it must have tired you.'

But their conversation had not tired Mariette.

'And your walk?'

'That has not either.'

'I am very glad.'

On the next day, therefore, the Curé proposed to his niece that she should accompany him as far as the cluster of houses occupied by the poor people who had been recipients of the Marquise's bounty. The young girl was afraid that it was rather far for her; but her uncle assuring her it was not, they set off together. They had not gone half-way before they were overtaken by a pretty little carriage drawn by two spirited horses, which M. Gaston de Saissières was driving.

'O M. le Curé,' said he, jumping down, 'why did you set off so early? I ought to have told you yesterday that I would come and fetch you with a carriage.'

He wanted the Curé and his niece to get in; but they refused, saying that they preferred to walk, Mariette especially.

'If your reason is that you may be freed from my presence,' said Gaston, laughing, 'it is trouble lost, for I shall accompany you on foot.'

He desired his coachman to follow, because, he said, they might, perhaps, be glad enough to make use of the carriage on their return. Only if he had anticipated the honour of conveying Mademoiselle Mariette, he would have chosen a more comfortable conveyance.

Mariette thanked him by a gesture, and said to herself, without knowing why, that she would walk until she was ready to drop, rather than get into any carriage whatever. The Marquis was as pleasant and as full of conversation as he had been the preceding evening. On their arrival at the hamlet inhabited by the poor people, he showed himself in a still more favourable light; for he gave evidence of possessing a great deal of benevolence and of good feeling; moreover he helped the Curé very adroitly in his inquiry. The result was not such as might have been desired. If amongst these people there were women and children worthy of the utmost pity, there were also husbands and fathers and brothers who were idle, drunken, even thieves perhaps, and certainly quite capable of having committed the deeds of which they had been accused.

'Things do not look promising,' said M. le Curé, as they were returning home. 'We cannot, in conscience, assure Madame de Saissières that these people are innocent. It is, unhappily, but too evident that the help she has so liberally given them without listening to my advice has encouraged them in idleness. We have a work to perform from the very beginning.

I have said so for a long time past. We must oblige these men to alter their way of life, and we must give nothing excepting to such as will consent to work. Meanwhile we must, of course, provide the women and children with the necessaries of life. All this requires care and attention. If you like, M. le Marquis, to take the business in hand, I am ready to help you.'

'I ask for nothing better,' said Gaston. 'These poor people will henceforth cease to belong to the Marquise, and will be transferred to me instead. It will be a loss for them as regards the amount of help I shall be able to give them, for my purse is but a light one. At any rate, however, I will give nothing away without your consent. If between us two we do not succeed in turning these people into saints, the devil will show himself to be very malicious.'

'The programme is a rather ambitious one,' said the Curé, laughing. 'I do not think we shall find amongst them the stuff out of which saints are made. In any case there is good to be done, therefore we must take it in hand. In the name of these unfortunate people, I accept your charity. Observe, however, that you are going to take upon yourself the care of several families, and that the burden may be a heavy one.'

'Bah!' exclaimed Gaston gaily. 'In case of need I will give up to you the whole of the allowance which my grandmother makes me; but it is not an enormous sum, I assure you. However, I am certain not to die of hunger. Madame de Saissières affords my servants, my horses, my dogs, and myself an unbounded hospitality. In this respect her liberality is unequalled. As to the rest, the provision made me is sufficient for my wants.'

'Then it is a settled thing,' said M. le Curé. 'We will say nothing more to the Marquise about the poor whom she has abandoned, but will form among ourselves a charitable association for helping and amending the culprits, until we can present them once more to her as worthy of her favour.'

Whilst thus talking they walked a little too quickly for Mariette, who did not think of complaining, so greatly was she interested in the subject of their conversation. But she was obliged to take her uncle's arm, and even the support thus afforded her was not sufficient; her strength failed her. Gaston begged her to get into the carriage. She refused, but she halted and sat down on the roadside.

'M. le Marquis,' said the Curé, 'I accept the carriage which you have been so good as to offer to my niece.'

In vain did the young girl still endeavour to refuse it. The Marquis made her get up—almost lifted her into the carriage, covered her with a mantle, and begged the Curé to take a seat beside her, saying that, as for himself, he would find his way on foot to the château, whilst his coachman would take them back to the presbytery. This arrangement was not agreed to. The coachman was desired to keep the horses at a walk, while the Curé kept on the right and the Marquis on the left of the vehicle; and so they proceeded on their way, both of them every moment asking the young girl how she felt. She answered that she was well—perfectly well. Wrapped up in the big mantle, in which her little person was almost lost, she felt vigour and warmth return to her. Very soon she wanted to get out and recommence her walk, but she was not allowed to do so; and so, in the liveliest manner possible, they continued their procession till they reached the presbytery. Then seeing the Marquis approaching the carriage, with the intention, perhaps, of taking her out like a child, and carrying her, all wrapped up as she was, into the house, Mariette slipped like an eel out of the mantle and the carriage, and appeared on the threshold, without any one being able to tell how she had got there.

The following day M. de Saissières came to the presbytery to inquire after Mariette's health, and to propose to the Curé that they should make another visit to the poor people whom they had seen the previous day. It was necessary, he said, that they should immediately take measures for helping the women and children, without it being possible that the aid thus afforded should be absorbed by the idle and vicious, whom it would be requisite they should oblige to work. Mariette felt quite well. For a long time past they had not seen her looking so blooming. They therefore proposed that she too should once more attempt the walk she had taken the morning before. The Marquis had this time brought with him a comfortable carriage, and one that was sufficiently large to hold three persons. But the young girl declined to go out.

'And this is the result of all your promises!' exclaimed her uncle. 'Is it because your yesterday's walk fatigued you too much?'

Mariette replied that she was tired, although she did not seem so, and persisted gently but firmly in her refusal. The Marquis wanted to put off the excursion until the following day, but Mariette would not consent, and pressed her uncle to set off. He did so, grumbling a little, and Gaston followed him, whilst Mariette went for a solitary walk into the garden of the presbytery. Although nothing had been done contrary to her wishes, she dried a few tears, which made her angry the while with herself, and all the more because she could not explain them.

A week passed by, during which, faithful to her promise, the young girl walked every day with her uncle. But she preferred to go out very early. The

Curé consented, although he said it was not as good for her; and as a proof that he was in the right, no matter how slowly they walked, Mariette was soon fatigued. Seeing her struggle against a lassitude which she vainly attempted to conceal, he brought her back to the house, and their short daily walks proved insufficient to restore her health.

'Walks which have no object are worth nothing,' he said to his niece. 'I should like to take you to-day to the hamlet of the "Forsaken." You know that is the title which M. de Saissières and I have given to the poor of the Marquise. Not so forsaken, after all, for the young Marquis is full of kindness towards them, and, thanks to the intelligent manner in which he performs his charities, he has already obtained some happy reforms. Come and see what they are, Mariette. Besides, your help is necessary to us. There are two or three women who are not deficient in courage or good works, but they stand in great need of the advice of my clever little housekeeper.'

Mariette did not reply 'No,' but would not let her uncle be accompanied by M. de Saissières. She would prefer to go alone with the Curé, she said, and they could then talk more freely.

'That excellent young man does not seem to me, to tell you the truth, to be very much in the way,' said the Curé. 'But if he wearies you, we will not say anything more about it. I do not think, however, that he is coming for me this afternoon.'

As there was a doubt about it, Mariette decided that they would make their visit some time during the morning. She reached the hamlet without much difficulty, and took an interest in visiting the families of which her uncle had spoken to her. There were a great many poor children in the cottages, who had nothing more than a few rags to cover them. She spoke kindly to the mothers, promised them some clothing materials, and on coming back said to her uncle that, in her opinion, it would be better to cease giving money, and to confine themselves solely to feeding and clothing the women and children.

'You are perfectly right,' said the Curé. 'It will be by far the best way in which to manage. But in order to do so your help is more than ever requisite.'

Mariette promised she would give her aid, and spoke with animation of some arrangements which would have to be made, whereby to insure the success of the work she had taken in hand. Then she became pensive, and, seeming to forget what she had said, looked very melancholy as she entered the presbytery.

However, pressed by her uncle, she set herself to work, and sent to the town for some coarse linen and warm woollen stuffs. Big Joseph was charged with the commission, which he was very glad to undertake, as Mariette herself had begged him to do so. Then calculating the needs of each household by the number and size of the children, she made up the materials into parcels, which were sent to the mothers with a message that Mariette would visit them shortly and look at the clothes after they were finished.

'But,' said the Curé, 'I must inform M. de Saissières of what we are doing, because I am using the money which he gave me for distribution in making these purchases.'

'It seems to me that it is needless to say anything about it to him just at present,' said Mariette. 'We are trying an experiment. Let us first see what will be the result of it. It is better to be silent until we do.'

'All that I can do to content you,' said her uncle, 'is not to write to the Marquis or to try and meet him. But if he comes I must tell him all. I do not like mysteries.'

Mariette did not insist. But she did not seem at all satisfied.

M. de Saissières came that day; unfortunately he had chosen his time badly. The Curé, who had been summoned to a sick person, had just gone out, and they did not know when he would return, because he had announced his intention of taking advantage of the opportunity of visiting some other sick parishioners. Mariette, still feeling fatigued after her excursion of the preceding day, was seated in her little room, shivering beside the stove, in which were burning a few little bits of charcoal. She was listening sadly to the wind, which was beating against the window, when Johanna came to tell her that the Marquis had asked whether mademoiselle knew when her uncle would be coming back.

'No, I really do not,' she said hastily. 'I think that it will be late before he returns.'

Johanna went out. She had hardly closed the door before Mariette called her back.

'M. de Saissières has not asked to see me?' she hesitatingly inquired.

'No, mademoiselle. But he is waiting in the passage. Will you not come down?'

'It is useless, Johanna. Tell M. de Saissières that, if he wishes, my uncle will make him a visit to-morrow at the château.'

Johanna obeyed. Mariette went to the window, and gently raised the curtain to see whether Gaston was leaving, and then, as though she reproached herself for her curiosity, she let it fall again, returned to her place beside the stove, and resumed some pressing piece of work which she had in hand, and which she ought already to have finished; it was an old soutane that required mending. But after her needle had flown feverishly along for some moments, it slackened its movements by little and little, and at last ceased entirely, the soutane fell to the ground, and Mariette remained motionless, her eyes fixed upon the fire. If she had still been at the window she would have seen Gaston standing irresolute in front of the house, and then setting off with visible impatience.

When the Curé returned, a long time afterwards,

'Well, Mariette,' he said, 'your secret has come out. I met M. de Saissières, and I told him what we were trying. He quite approved of it, on the one condition that we should continue—that is to say, that you should continue—to superintend the different families.'

'But—' exclaimed Mariette.

'There are no "buts" about it, my child. It is a good work which is in question, and you cannot withdraw. The Marquis sees quite well, he says, that the best thing he can do is not to interfere any more in it, and to let you act. He will put into my hands all his alms, in order that we may dispose of them according to your ideas. I think that every one will be benefited, the poor above all; for M. de Saissières, encouraged, doubtless, by the certainty that his money will be well employed, has just given me some more, in fact all that he had, so that we are now quite rich.'

When they next visited the hamlet of the 'Forsaken,' they were grieved to find that Mariette's idea had not been productive of any very wonderful results. Few, very few, clothes had been made. Amongst the children, one had on a shirt which did not go below his waist, another had a frock which gave her the look of a half-empty sack of potatoes, the third had a pair of trousers which were a great deal too long; the mothers had, however, taken a little better care of themselves. However, they had not done much, and yet all the materials, they said, had been used.

'Yes, used! Sold for twopence, and drank by the husbands,' said the Curé, taking a pinch of snuff.

Uncle and niece looked at each other with a disappointed air. Evidently it was necessary they should exercise a daily superintendence. Mariette scolded a little, threatened to have nothing more to do with the people, and received in return the fairest possible promises.

'M. de Saissières will not be able to congratulate us on the success we have obtained,' said she, whilst they were on their way back to the presbytery.

'No,' said the Curé; 'yet when he was giving them money, did things go on any better?'

'I do not know, uncle. But at any rate these people had all the money then which M. de Saissières gave, whilst in reselling the clothing materials they will only receive a very small portion of what the things cost us. How I regret that I ever allowed myself to give any advice! But now that we have once begun, let us try to do as little harm as possible.'

'Quite right, my child. That is the way in which you ought to speak. Get some more material, give each of these women her appointed task, and watch over the execution of it yourself, making, if it should be necessary, daily visits to them.'

Mariette promised, and she kept her word. Closely superintended as they now were, the women got on better, and were not able to sell the materials which were given them. The aspect of the hamlet quickly changed. There were no longer to be seen any women in rags, no longer any naked children. Even in the poorest houses there was something which resembled neatness and order. The Curé was enchanted. He regretted that the Marquis de Saissières had given up his visits to the 'Forsaken.' He would have liked to show him what they had succeeded in making of his *protégés*. But Mariette did not wish that he should be spoken to about it. Above all, she was opposed to her uncle's proposal that he should be asked to revisit the hamlet.

In spite of her being still very weak and suffering, the young girl went there every day. She always found strength enough to go that distance, although she was obliged to take a considerable time over her walk; but in the end she reached the hamlet, and after taking a long rest there, succeeded in getting back on foot to the presbytery.

Amongst the families whom she visited and directed, there was one which particularly interested her. It consisted not only of a good gentle woman, of five fine children who had not been prevented by poverty from growing as fast as cabbages, but also—a very rare circumstance in the little colony—of a father who made an honest livelihood, instead of subsisting, like his good-for-nothing neighbours, by thieving and poaching. Employed in the town, he spent his days there. If he did not earn much, he brought home, at any rate, every evening, a contented mind and the good-humour of a man who has employed his time well.

CHAPTER X.

ONE day, when Mariette and her uncle were going to the hamlet, a peasant overtook them, and, quite out of breath, begged that the Curé would go with him at once to his mother, as she was at the point of death.

'Quick, M. le Curé, if you please.'

'Certainly, friend, I will set off this moment. We will go to her as fast as we can.'

The Curé cast a look of perplexity at his poor little niece, who was walking with difficulty.

'Go, uncle,' she said; 'do not trouble yourself about me. We are only two steps from Catherine's house. I will go as far as there, and rest, after which I will return to the presbytery.'

'Alone!' he exclaimed. 'No, you shall not.'

'Well, then, I will get Catherine to accompany me. I promise you I will.'

The Curé hesitated. But he had no time to deliberate. Pressed by Mariette, and adjured by the peasant, he set off, a little against his inclination, may God forgive him! Turning his head, he looked at his niece as he hurried along.

'Supposing I were to come back for you here?' he said.

'Don't think of it, uncle,' she replied. 'Go in peace, I beg. I shall doubtless be at home long before you.'

'Be prudent, and do not walk too fast,' he exclaimed once more before he disappeared at the turning of the road.

Mariette then walked on to the hamlet, and visited one or two families, after which she went to 'her friends,' as she called them. She was very tired, and gladly accepted the chair that they offered her beside the fire, which was very economically kept up, but sufficiently so for the season, which was still rather cold. After having gone into several little details concerning the family, and kissing the children, who were clean and neatly dressed, thanks to her, she administered some kind advice to the mother, a good and honest woman, who listened to her attentively. Then the Curé's niece placed upon the iron bar in front of the fire her little feet, which were almost lost in her coarse woollen stockings and country shoes. Overcome by fatigue she put her elbows on her knees, and, supporting her chin in her white thin hands, gazed pensively at the beech-roots which smouldered on the hearth. What were the thoughts which lay concealed behind her dreamy brow? What were the feelings which made her eyes so sad? Regret for the past? Weariness of the present? The emptiness of the future? Yes, it was all that. And, perhaps, other things besides. But nothing in the profound melancholy which had taken possession of the poor child was in the least akin to despair or even to discouragement. If life were void of pleasures, destitute of joys, without promise, she beheld beyond it another future, which already, like a distant aurora, vaguely illuminated the sad and mournful path along which she was patiently walking without uttering a complaint, weighed down beneath the burden of her wretchedness.

How long a time had Mariette been lost in thought? The children were playing quietly in a corner, the mother was knitting in silence, a little dog seated on the threshold of the door broke out from time to time into a melancholy bark, the beech-roots crackled upon the ashes, and the young girl's heart was far away, very far—perhaps it had even ascended very high.

'What o'clock is it?' she asked all at once, as though she were waking from a dream.

There was not any clock in the house, and Mariette had no watch, for the charming little plaything inscribed with her initials, which had been given her long ago by her father, and which had marked so many happy hours, had been sold with everything else. Since then she would not have another watch. There was in the presbytery a great big clock, by which every one in the house regulated the distribution of the day. That was sufficient. But just now a watch would have been useful. The light, which was rapidly decreasing, made Mariette feel that she had remained longer than she ought to have done, and that it was necessary she should at once set off.

'Will you walk with me until we get in sight of the presbytery?' Mariette asked Catherine.

'Of course, mademoiselle, immediately.'

'But the children?'

'They will stay here.'

'Alone, without any one to look after them?'

'Yes, it will not signify in the least.'

'I have very often forbidden you to leave your children. Take them to some neighbour's house.'

'There is only one who would be willing to take charge of them, and she is not at home. I saw her go out a little while ago. But what could happen to the children?'

'A great many things. They might go too near the fire. How can one tell? My good woman, I will not allow you to leave them in that way. You promised me that you would never do it.'

'This time it is for your sake, mademoiselle, since it is you whom I am going to accompany.'

'I will not allow you, on my account, to do anything which ought not to be done. I will wait until your husband comes back.'

'But it will be quite dark before he returns.'

'That is true. How is it I did not think of it all when I promised my uncle that I would ask you to take me back? If I wait much longer he will return before me, and it will make him uneasy not to find me home; yet, tired as he is certain to be by his long walk, he will come and meet me. That must not be. I will return alone.'

Mariette, in fact, set off, reproaching herself for having through thoughtlessness rendered impossible the keeping of the promise she had made her uncle. Proceeding as well as she could, she had not got half-way before, having quite exhausted her strength, she was obliged to sit down on the roadside to take breath, and noticed with regret that it was becoming dark: not that she was frightened, but she knew that her uncle did not like her to be out alone at night in the country. Instinctively she looked with questioning eyes up and down the road until she saw a human form approaching her from the direction in which the hamlet was situated, and another coming to her from the village towards which she was journeying. She imagined at first that it was her uncle, but she soon perceived that it was some one who had neither his figure nor his walk, nor above all his soutane. As to the person who was coming from the hamlet, and who was walking very fast, it was not difficult to guess that it was Catherine's husband, who, having come back to the house sooner than usual, must have been sent after her, with instructions to overtake her as soon as possible. Not wishing to let him get out of breath, Mariette rose, and, advancing towards him, exclaimed,.

'Do not be in such a hurry. I am here.'

'Ah, mademoiselle, how glad I am that I have been able to overtake you!' was the rejoinder.

But the voice was that of Gaston de Saissières, and at the same moment the Marquis—for it was really himself in person—advanced towards Mariette and bowed. Surprised and confused, she drew back.

'You are quite astonished to see me, are you not?' said he. 'I must explain. But first, accept my arm. I will take you home. I have just come from the woman whom you have been visiting. She told me that she had not been allowed to accompany you. I will replace her. It is impossible you can traverse this road alone. Night is coming on.'

'I am not a child, I am not afraid of the dark. I shall have reached home before night has come on. Thank you, M. le Marquis.'

'Which means to say, Mademoiselle Mariette, that you do not wish for my company?'

'Pardon me, M. le Marquis, but I cannot accept it.'

'Why?'

'I do not wish you to trouble yourself on my account.'

'Trouble myself! and in what way? Do not our respective roads lie in almost the same direction, yours to the presbytery and mine to the château?'

'No—yes—perhaps. But I shall delay you. I do not like to do so.'

'I am not at all pressed for time. Besides, did you not tell me you count on getting back before night? If so you walk very fast.'

'I was wrong to say so. On the contrary, I walk very slowly.'

'Then you will not be able to get back before night. It is another reason why I should accompany you.'

'Permit me, monsieur, to beg you will do nothing of the kind. I am in no need of your escort. I thank you a thousand times for your kindness. You were walking very fast when I so stupidly stopped you. Continue, I beg of you, at the same pace, and as though you had never met me.'

'Pardon, pardon, I did not *meet* you, mademoiselle. I *overtook* you, which is quite a different matter. I was certainly walking very fast—indeed I fancy that I must have run; but it was after you I was running. Do not you see, then, that I am not at all inclined to obey you? I shall not leave you until we have reached the presbytery, and until I have consigned you, safe and sound, into the hands of your uncle.'

M

It was all said so naturally, and with so much gaiety, that Mariette had not a word to reply. She stood still, hesitated, and seemed almost annoyed.

'Is it possible you can be astonished, mademoiselle, that I will not leave you alone, at nightfall, upon this solitary road? In fact, I cannot understand your refusal. Be so good as to take my arm.'

These last words had been pronounced with perfect politeness, but also with the air of a person of too high rank to think for a moment of expecting anything but acceptance of his kindness.

Mariette leant her hand upon the arm which was offered her. At that moment the individual whom she had seen approaching in the opposite direction from that along which the Marquis had come, drew near.

'Mamselle Mariette,' he said, 'it is me—Joseph. I have come for you. Johanna is uneasy about you. M. le Curé told her that he was going to take the Blessed Sacrament to a woman who was ill, and that you were coming home. But as you did not come, Johanna got into such a state! She called to me and said, "Joseph, go and see what has become of our young lady." So I set off.'

'You have run very fast, my good Joseph; you are quite out of breath. And poor Johanna, who is letting herself be anxious! Come, let us make haste. M. le Marquis,' said she, hesitating a little, 'you see I am no longer alone. This good fellow will accompany me home. I have only to thank you a thousand times for your kindness in wishing—'

'What!' exclaimed Gaston, surprised, 'are you going to let that boy take you home?'

'Yes. We are old acquaintances, and I could not have, in case of need, a more determined or more devoted defender.'

'That is as much as to say I am of no use,' answered Gaston. 'I will leave you, then. Good-evening, mademoiselle.'

He bowed and went on his way, with a step which, although it was not hurried, was sufficiently quick for him soon to have left Mariette behind. She made a gesture as though she wished to recall him; then, recollecting herself, she said,

'Come, my good Joseph, let us return to the presbytery.'

So they proceeded on their way. In front of them Gaston was still walking very fast. If he had looked back, and if he had seen with what difficulty the young girl dragged herself along, he would doubtless have returned in order to offer her once more his arm. But he did not look back. He was already at a considerable distance from them, and in fact was just going to disappear in the twilight.

'Joseph,' exclaimed Mariette hastily, 'please run after M. le Marquis, and tell him that I beg him to have the kindness to wait a moment, as I have something to say to him.'

Seeing that he did not at once obey,

'Why do you not set off?' she inquired.

Joseph soon overtook M. de Saissières, who, hearing some one behind him, had stood still. After receiving the message, he returned to Mariette.

'You asked for me, mademoiselle?' he said, in a gentle tone.

Mariette was agitated, and felt as though she would have been glad not to have recalled him.

'Yes,' she said, hesitating; 'I wanted—I was afraid—I fancied—'

'What did you fancy?' asked Gaston, with interest. 'Can I be of any use to you? Are you ill?'

'No, no; I am quite well, thank you; but I regret—'

'What do you regret, mademoiselle?'

'To have stopped you. Continue your walk, I beg. I ought not—'

'In point of fact,' exclaimed the young man, laughing, 'if it were not that I believe you to be incapable of even seeming to be inspired by the spirit of mischief, I should imagine that you were wanting to amuse yourself at my expense. Do I look as if I were in such a hurry that you must be continually excusing yourself for detaining me? You called me back because you had something to say to me. Here I am. I will stay beside you until you please to explain yourself.'

Mariette felt that she had placed herself in a ridiculous position. She made a great effort, and said, with simplicity,

'It is you, M. le Marquis, who have good cause to amuse yourself just now at my expense, for I am very absurd. The truth is, I am afraid that I seemed very insensible of your goodness. It was indeed most kind in you to wish to accompany me. I did not thank you as I ought to have done, and I am very sorry. That, however, is all I wished to say to you.'

There was something very touching in the mixture of simplicity and dignity apparent in the young girl's manner. Gaston was struck by it.

'It made me happy to offer you my services, mademoiselle,' he said. 'You had no need of them; you declined them. Nothing is more simple. I then left you. Is not that very simple also?'

'If it be really as simple as that,' said Mariette, smiling, 'I have again been in the wrong in stopping you when you were going on your way. Forgive me, and good-evening, monsieur.'

'O, no, indeed!' cried Gaston. 'This time it is not quite as simple. I forewarn you that if, after having called me back, you dismiss me again, you will offend me mortally.'

'I have a great mind to run the risk!' exclaimed Mariette, carried away by the natural vivacity of her character.

'No, no!' said Gaston, in the same tone. 'It would distress me to have any cause of complaint against you. Thanks to your page in clogs, you do not require me any longer. If I accompany you, it is because it gives me pleasure to do so. Moreover, I don't intend to leave you until we have reached the door of the presbytery. Be so kind as to take my arm.'

Mariette was obliged to take the arm which had been so courteously offered her for the second time, and they set off. Big Joseph, whistling one of his insane airs, walked for some time in front of them. Then all at once, vexed, doubtless, at seeing he was of no use, he went off without its being possible to say what had become of him. Besides, they had not been thinking enough about him to have remarked his disappearance. The two young people talked gaily together. Gaston told her how he had attentively followed, without the Curé or Mariette suspecting it, the progress of the reformation which had been worked in the hamlet of the 'Forsaken,' as he had gone there almost daily; and how, when he saw uncle and niece coming, he had hidden himself, from fear of startling them; how also on that day, seeing Mariette set off alone, he had gone as fast as he could to Catherine's house, to ask whether the Curé were ill; and how, finally, after having heard that Mariette would not allow any one to accompany her, he had run after her to offer his services. Mariette, for a moment forgetting the restraint to which her life was subjected, gave herself up to the charm of a conversation which recalled to her remembrance the society in which she had been brought up. She replied to Gaston with animation. She was not conscious of fatigue. They proceeded slowly along their way. Gaston was astonished to find he took so much pleasure in talking with this little girl. However, at last they reached the presbytery.

'Ah, here we are, at home,' said Gaston. 'It is very odd that I feel as though we had been walking only five minutes.'

Mariette might have said the same thing, but she did not. She requested Gaston to go in with her, for she did not wish their meeting should wear an air of mystery. Just as they were about to knock at the door, the Curé showed himself.

'Here you are, at last, my darling!' he exclaimed. 'I was greatly alarmed at not finding you at home on my return. Spite of Johanna wanting to prevent me from going after you, on the pretext that she had sent Joseph, I was just on the point of setting out.'

He made a gesture of surprise on seeing the

Marquis, whose arm Mariette had designedly retained.

'If I had only had Joseph,' she said, 'I should have been on the road still. It is entirely owing to my having been able to take the Marquis's arm that I have walked so quickly.'

She really fancied that she had been walking fast. The road had seemed to her very short.

The Marquis was persuaded to go in. They installed themselves in the little square sitting-room, where Johanna had fortunately made a fire, thinking that her master and her young mistress, tired as they doubtless would be on their return, would sup more comfortably and be warmer there than in the kitchen. The table had already been laid. Seeing that Gaston seemed about to take leave at once, there was a moment's awkwardness; Mariette looked at her uncle, and wondered if he would ask the young man to share in their humble repast. Casting his eyes on the old wooden clock which was ticking in a corner of the room,

'You will hardly be able to reach the château in time for dinner, M. le Marquis,' said the Curé.

'You are right,' said Gaston, laughing, 'seeing that at this very moment my grandmother, who is punctuality personified, is sitting down to table. She knows that I am sometimes tempted to take a long walk, and she does not wait for me.'

'And your absence will not make her uneasy?'

'No, certainly not. In this respect I enjoy entire liberty.'

'That being the case, I will beg you, in all simplicity, to exchange for this one evening the fare of the château for that of the presbytery; if, indeed, you should not lose too much by doing so.'

'If I had dared, I would have already asked your permission,' said Gaston.

Mariette wished she could have thanked him for answering so simply and kindly. Throwing down his cap, which he had until then held in his hand, the young man was about to sit down at once to the table.

'Not so quick,' said the Curé, laughing. 'Let us allow Mariette time to go into the kitchen and see that we are not likely absolutely to die of hunger, and let us also permit Johanna to set an earthenware plate and an iron fork there for you.'

'If Mademoiselle Mariette leaves the fireside, where she is so comfortably settled, I shall take it for granted my presence disturbs you, and I will make my escape. As to the plate and fork, I should dearly like to spare Johanna the trouble of getting them, and fetch them myself.'

M. de Saissières seemed to wish, by his gaiety and the simplicity of his manner, to obtain forgiveness for having intruded into so primitive an abode. It was with a mixture of embarrassment, and of another feeling which bore a rather near resemblance to gratitude, that Mariette saw the elegant Marquis take his share in their simple repast, with as much appetite and pleasure as he had ever found in a more luxurious diet. Although the bill of fare was certainly not very complicated, they remained a long time at table. Gaston exhibited, with perfect tact and an entire absence of self-consciousness, all the graces of a genial and brilliant character. Carried away, almost intoxicated, Mariette involuntarily allowed herself to be drawn into the current of conversation, and nothing could then be stranger than the contrast between her homely attire and her correct, spirited, and elegant language. The Curé himself became animated, and took part in their conversation. He introduced into the most trivial subjects reflections, the refinement and depth of which were all the more striking, because the form in which they were couched was simple and original, and the expressions of which he made use happy, concise, and picturesque. Never had a humble repast, never had a village presbytery, been enlivened by such a conversation. At last they left the table, and, seating themselves by the fireside, still went on talking. The old wooden clock in vain struck the hour; no one heard it. The evening was drawing quickly to a close. At last the Curé fortunately cast his eyes on the face of the clock.

'Nine o'clock!' he exclaimed. 'Nine o'clock! I could not have believed it.'

Gaston could not believe it either; nor Mariette. But the Curé declared that the clock was right. He proved it was so, by comparing it with his own large silver watch.

'It is our hour for retiring,' said he. 'Nay, it is even past the time. M. le Marquis, what will madame, your grandmother, say? You must start at once. Nevertheless, since you have been so good as to share in our supper, you must now take part in our night prayers.'

Johanna, being summoned, prayers were quickly said. Gaston, kneeling down by the side of Mariette, was exceedingly devout. Then, after making the sign of the cross in a most edifying manner, he seemed inclined to remain yet a little while longer. But the Curé held out his hand to him.

'After prayers the day is at an end, M. le Marquis. Have the kindness to present my compliments to Madame la Marquise.'

Gaston at last withdrew, after having cordially clasped M. le Curé's hand and respectfully pressed Mariette's. As soon as he had departed an inexplicable change took place in the room. A moment before it had seemed as though it had been a pretty drawing-room, full of light and gaiety; Gaston gone, it was nothing more than a poor little parlour, hardly lighted by a modest lamp, empty and sad even unto death.

Mariette, standing, and with a smile still upon her lips, cast around her an astonished gaze. The severe aspect which everything bore brought her back to reality. She uttered a stifled sigh, put her hands to her brow, as though she were waking from a dream; trembled, and slowly retired, without looking behind her. The Curé came and wished her good-night; contrary to his usual habit, he did so in very few words. He seemed to be preoccupied, or perhaps it was only that he was tired, after having talked and sat up later than he was accustomed to do.

CHAPTER XI.

THIS memorable supper had taken place on a Saturday. The next morning the bell was ringing for Mass, but Mariette had not yet come down-stairs. Johanna was waiting for her, with her hood upon her head. When the young girl made her appearance she was so pale, her eyes bore the trace of so many tears, that the faithful servant uttered an exclamation of surprise, and asked her if she were ill. Mariette answered briefly in the negative, adding that it was necessary to hurry to church.

After Mass they breakfasted, the Curé looking meanwhile at his niece through the corner of his eye. Johanna, who was at table with them, and who had the gift of swallowing a cup of coffee at one draught and of making but one mouthful of a slice of bread, always finished very quickly. Putting back her chair against the wall, she went out to busy herself about her usual occupations, whilst uncle and niece remained together *tête-à-tête*. The Curé taking the young girl's hand,

'My child,' he said, ' you are ill.'

'No, uncle,' she replied, in a weak voice.

'Sad, then, very sad,' he said tenderly.

Mariette was going to reply in the negative, when she was prevented by a scruple. She remained silent.

'Have you nothing to say to me?'

'No, uncle; I feel a little overcome. Do not pay any attention to me; I shall be better soon.'

'I hope so, Mariette. I am afraid that you over-tired yourself a little yesterday. We had intended, you know, to go again to the hamlet to-day; but I do not think you are strong enough to undertake such a walk.'

'No,' said Mariette emphatically; 'I could not, in fact. If you will permit me, uncle, I will not go out.'

'Quite right, my child. I will inform M. de Saissières that the walk is put off until to-morrow. You remember he asked if he might meet us there to-day.'

'I earnestly beg, uncle, that you will not send any message to the château, but go without me to the hamlet.'

'Why? There is no hurry. What does a delay of twenty-four hours signify?'

'I shall not be any better able to go to the hamlet to-morrow than I am to-day. Besides, my presence is of no consequence.'

'You are not really in earnest. Are you already

thinking of abandoning the task you had undertaken, and which you were performing so well ?'

'Uncle, I entreat you to allow me to stay away from the hamlet for some little time.'

Mariette's agitation contrasted too strongly with the habitual repose of her manner for the Curé not to be struck by it. However, he merely said,

'It shall be as you wish. I will go without you.'

Accordingly in the afternoon he set off alone. Mariette punctually performed all the household duties she had been accustomed to fulfil; after which she retired to her own room. But she found herself unable to remain there. To sew or to read was equally impossible. Although she was overcome by fatigue, she went into the little garden for a walk. But very soon the pacing up and down within four walls became a torture to her. Excited, and her head on fire, she returned to the house. In the passage she found herself face to face with Gaston, who had just entered.

'I am delighted to see you, mademoiselle,' he said joyously. 'I was afraid you were ill when I saw M. le Curé going out alone. First of all, a thousand pardons for the manner in which I have intruded upon you. I found the door open, and no Johanna to speak to. I am therefore obliged to ask you myself whether you will allow me to pay you my respects.'

Mariette did not answer; but Gaston opened the door of the little sitting-room for her, as she still stood on the threshold.

'Are you not coming in, mademoiselle?' he said. 'But perhaps you prefer to return to the garden.'

Gaston did not seem to have the most distant idea that his visit might perhaps be unacceptable.

'Monsieur,' said Mariette, 'I think my uncle has gone to the hamlet in the expectation of finding you there.'

'That is impossible, mademoiselle; for I am certain I told M. le Curé that I would come here for him. He cannot be expecting to find me there.'

'But you might overtake him.'

'It would not be easy. I saw him set off, and he was walking very fast.'

'It was doubtless because he wanted to overtake you as soon as possible.'

'I do not think so. In any case, what does it signify? I will go to the hamlet when M. le Curé is returning from it; in that way we shall be sure to meet, and the misunderstanding can be explained.'

So speaking Gaston waited, with a smile upon his lips, until Mariette should decide for either the parlour or the garden. The young girl made a movement as if she were about to enter the sitting-room; then she changed her mind.

'I should prefer the garden,' she murmured.

'I think you are right,' said Gaston; 'the weather is fine, although it is a little cold.'

Mariette hesitated, and glanced at him. He seemed so firmly determined to remain, that she saw no way of avoiding his visit; so she went into the garden, and they walked up and down side by side. Gaston at first seemed to be greatly interested in the culture of the fruit and vegetables. Thinking, doubtless, that such a subject of conversation must be agreeable to the Curé's niece, he continued to indulge in it. But when the young girl, soon becoming incapable of replying to his questions, confessed that she understood nothing at all about gardening,

'You are just like me!' he exclaimed. 'It bores me terribly. There is nothing I should like better than to leave the cabbages on one side.'

Preoccupied though she was, Mariette could not help remarking the ingenuous answer of the Marquis; it signified, in fact, that he had at first imagined these vulgar cabbages which bored him so much were quite worthy of occupying the young girl's attention. Without being conscious of it, something like a smile flitted across her lips. Gaston perceived it, and seeing, with the promptitude of a man of the world, the little awkwardness of which he had been guilty, he attempted to repair it.

'You are smiling, mademoiselle?'

'No,' answered Mariette, unconscious of the fib.

'O, yes, you are smiling at me; and you are right, for I have made myself very ridiculous.'

'I do not know what you mean. In any case, you give me credit for a great deal too much cleverness.'

'It would be impossible to do so. Will you allow me to tell you why you smiled?'

'It is not necessary,' Mariette promptly answered.

'Now you are betraying yourself,' exclaimed Gaston.

Mariette, this time, laughed outright, whilst Gaston assumed a serious expression.

'I am asking myself,' he said, 'what penance the Curé will impose when you let him know that you have told a story, as you have just been doing.'

The quickness with which the smiling expression disappeared from Mariette's face warned Gaston that his pleasantry had not been in the best possible taste.

'What can I be about to-day?' he said, in a different tone; 'I am uttering nothing but nonsense. Just now I was talking to you about cabbages, as though they were the only subject of conversation which could give you any pleasure; and now I have given way to what is, to say the least, but a very poor kind of joke. I am going, however, to tell you why I am so stupid—it is that I am not at ease. I fancy that I perceive—tell me that I am mistaken—but I do feel as though my presence were a little disagreeable to you.'

Without knowing it, Mariette made a gesture of denial.

'I was deceiving myself, then,' said Gaston. 'So much the better. It would be impossible for me to tell you how delighted I am to find myself once more in your society. I passed a charming evening yesterday, Mademoiselle Mariette; such an evening as I have never spent before, I confess. Is it so easy, then, to amuse oneself? I could not have believed it. I assure you I am telling you all this quite simply, just as it presents itself to my mind. Do not you think it is very strange that I should speak to you with such freedom? There is something about you which impels me—which inspires me with confidence: it seems to me that if I had a sister—'

'It would indeed be strange,' said Mariette, interrupting him, 'if whilst walking up and down between beds of cabbages and onions, with the niece of a country Curé, you were to assume the tone and the language which would be suitable to a drawing-room and towards a woman of the world.'

'That is true, in at least so far that I should never think of speaking to you of the trivial matters which would doubtless form the subject of my conversation with the woman of the world in question. On the other side, it would be just as impossible for me to speak to you as I should to a young country girl who was perfectly—what shall I say?—completely rustic, and whose horizon was limited by the walls of her garden or the boundaries of her village.'

'And yet, just now, you were speaking to me very zealously about cabbages!'

'Do not take advantage of my stupidity. I repeat that there is something in you which is quite peculiar, and which makes one never—'

Mariette, as though displeased that Gaston should continue to speak of herself, asked him whether it would not be better for him to go and meet the Curé, who must have doubtless left the hamlet by this time, and be on his way back.

'No,' said the Marquis, 'he can hardly have got there. But since you have spoken of the hamlet, mademoiselle, let us say one word about our poor people. I have not, as yet, congratulated you upon the success you have obtained; you alone were capable of working such a miracle. Without having any suspicion of it yourself, I have almost daily admired you in your works, and, under your inspiration, I have conceived great projects. I will not speak to you of them now. But to-morrow, when we are going together to the hamlet, we will talk about them —that is to say, I will very humbly submit my ideas to you. If you approve of them, we will all work together towards their realisation—you will see it will be something magnificent, for with your help, and under your direction, success is certain.'

'You do me too much honour, M. le Marquis.'

'No, no, pardon; let us see. What time will suit you best for me to come and take you to-morrow?'

'I beg you will speak of your projects to my uncle.'

'But it is your opinion that I want. As for him, you know quite well that anything you may decide upon will be right in his eyes. Tell me, then, at what o'clock I may call for you with the carriage.'

'But,' said Mariette, 'I do not think of going to the hamlet to-morrow.'

'O, very well; the day after, then?'

'The last walks which I took there tired me so much, that I do not intend to resume them so soon again.'

'These are sad tidings, mademoiselle. Sad for me and for the poor people also.'

'I do not see that at all. Go to the hamlet to-morrow with my uncle, and tell him of your projects.'

'No,' said Gaston firmly. 'I will not go to the hamlet unless you will go also. And as to my projects, if you will not allow me to tell you about them, I will think of them no more.'

Mariette looked at him with surprise.

'It seems to me that it is very natural I should not,' he said. 'I began to really interest myself in my poor people, and to busy myself about them only when you had begun to interest yourself, on your side, in their behalf. I fancy you no longer wish to do so. Well, then, I do not either.'

'You are jesting, M. le Marquis,' said Mariette rather coldly, for she felt an ever-increasing desire to shorten Gaston's visit.

'Not at all. I will give M. le Curé as much money as he thinks it right to ask for the poor people; but I will never set foot again in the hamlet, unless you will go there also.'

Mariette did not answer, and, without any sign of affectation, directed her steps towards the house.

'Are you going in?' asked Gaston.

'Yes,' answered Mariette.

He offered her his arm. She refused it. They entered the house in silence. Mariette paused in the little passage in order to make the Marquis understand that she desired to receive his farewells.

'You are going to dismiss me?' he asked.

'Forgive me for reminding you that my uncle is waiting for you.'

Gaston bowed and went to the front door. Just as he was going to open it, he returned towards the young girl.

'It is ridiculous,' he said, 'but it is impossible for me to go away in this manner. You seem annoyed. Have I displeased you in any way, mademoiselle?'

'Not in the least,' said Mariette, agitated.

As Gaston stood still casting upon her an indefinable glance, she suddenly bowed to him, saying, 'Good-morning, M. le Marquis,' in a tone which showed it was this time meant to be a formal *congé* which she was giving him.

'Very well. No!' cried the young man, 'I will not leave you thus. I see perfectly well that something has taken place between you and me to-day, which has displeased you. If I have been in the wrong, I wish to apologise. Besides, I have something else to say to you. You are prejudiced against me, Mademoiselle Mariette; I understand it, and I have no right to be surprised. You avoid me as much as you can. I see it is because you are afraid of meeting me that you are depriving my grandmother of the pleasure of seeing you at the château. But are you not a little severe? You are more so than any one else is—more than your uncle, who does not show any such aversion from me. "What does it signify to you?" you will perhaps say. But it is no use to ask me that. I value your good opinion, and am capable of great efforts in order to render it favourable.'

The accent of simplicity and of truth with which Gaston spoke impressed Mariette, rendering her position still more difficult, and she blushed deeply. But feeling, at the same moment, that she must not allow herself to exhibit the slightest appearance of emotion, which might lend any importance to the language employed by the young man, and resolved, with the promptitude and clear judgment which characterised her, to prevent all possibility of any misconception,

'M. le Marquis,' she said, in a tone which was serious, and which in spite of herself was sad, 'I will not ask you if you are jesting. To do so would be, it seems to me, to inflict some injury on us both. You tell me that you attach a value to my opinion. It would, perhaps, be proper to answer that it is not worth the respect you pay to it. But I feel that you wish to acquire the esteem of all honest hearts. If I judged you a little severely at first, I was in the wrong. Now, my uncle, your grandmother, all who come in contact with you, render you justice. I do the same. Let this assurance suffice you. A little reflection will enable you to understand that the kind of intimacy with which you are so good as to wish to honour me is not possible between us. Do not oblige me to arm myself with the coldness of which you complain. There can be nothing in common between the Marquis de Saissières and the Curé's niece.'

Gaston made a movement as though he were about to utter a protest. She stopped him by a gesture.

'Adieu now,' she said. 'Leave me, I beg.'

The young man looked at her for a moment.

'You are right,' he said. 'I am going. Will you permit me to shake hands with you?'

She shook her head.

He bowed to her with a respect with which no woman had ever before been able to inspire him, and the moment afterwards the door of the presbytery closed between them.

CHAPTER XII.

'MIGHT I ask, Gaston, whether the battle you are waging against that log is going to last much longer?' asked Madame de Saissières, who, reclining in her easy-chair, her hands crossed upon her knees, was watching her grandson seated opposite her at the other side of the fireplace. Mechanically, a poker in his hand, he was fighting with an obstinate log of wood. His grandmother's question made him start; then giving a last blow to the log, which answered him with a volley of sparks, he laid down the poker, leaned back in his chair, and kept silence.

'I did not intend to deprive you of a pleasure,' his grandmother said, in a slightly sarcastic tone. 'Do not let me prevent you from continuing to indulge in it.'

'To tell the truth, the pleasure was but slight. It costs me nothing to give it up.'

'However slight it be it is better than nothing,' went on the Marquise, in the same ironical tone.

Gaston did not reply. After some moments' silence, Madame de Saissières, bending a little towards him, said, with a smile,

'You are being cruelly bored here, my child.'

'Not in the least so, madame, I assure you.'

'Madame!' she repeated. 'How ceremonious we are! Have we come to *that?*'

'I ought to have said "mother!"' exclaimed the young man affectionately. 'It was a slip of the tongue.'

'Ah, that is all right. But now, my son, let us speak seriously. The life you are leading here weighs upon you; it is almost insupportable.'

'When have I ever complained?'

'Never, it is true, Gaston. But the *ennui* you feel shows itself, in spite of you, in a manner which is very evident.'

'And all that arises from a few blows given to a log by a poker,' said Gaston, smiling.

'Not at all. The poker and the log have neither of them taught me anything I did not know before. I have seen for a long time past what is the state of your feelings. Do not deny it, my son; what is the use? You would not be able to deceive me. I notice you more than you imagine. During the last fortnight especially you have been waging a hard battle with yourself. Such a state of things cannot continue. I am not as unreasonable as you suppose. I understand that an existence like that which we lead may become a torment to a young man of your character. I cannot bear to see you unhappy, Gaston. Three months ago, when I snatched you from the fatal influence which was an incubus, weighing down your life, I did indeed require a promise from you not to leave me without my permission; but it was not a selfish requirement on my part. Whatever may be the pleasure I take in your society, I have never thought of condemning you to mine.'

'Condemning me! O mother, what an expression!'

'Do not let us dwell upon words. They are of no importance. Let us go straight to the object I have in view. Observe that I do not address any questions to you. Do not, then, fear that you will have to pain me by an avowal. You have none to make. It does not depend upon you to bring about any change. In other words, spite of your wish to satisfy me—I firmly believe in the perfect sincerity of your desire—you cannot be happy here with me. Well, Gaston, you must leave me—you must quit the château.'

The young man shook his head by way of refusal.

'Do not be childish,' pursued the old lady, in a decided tone. 'You shall leave me; I have come to the decision that you must. You shall travel during some months—for a longer time, even, if you wish. When the desire arises in your heart to see your grandmother again, you can come back.'

Gaston remained silent for some time, his forehead buried in his hands. Then rising, he said,

'I accept your offer, mother. If you had not been the first to speak I should never have told you the state of my feelings. But since you perceive it so clearly, what is the use of attempting concealment? It is true I am not happy. You speak of *ennui*. It is not that. It would be impossible to describe what I feel. In spite of your kindness towards me—in spite of the profound gratitude with which it inspires me— there are moments in which life is a burden to me. Since you are so good as to permit me, I will travel a little. I shall soon come back to you in a better frame of mind, and I shall have the happiness of finding you well and strong as ever. That you may be quite convinced I am not going away in order that I may recommence the sort of life with which, thanks to you, I have definitely broken, we will settle my route together. I will follow it out to the letter.'

Grandmother and grandson prolonged their conversation, and the route was settled. Madame de Saissières decided that Gaston's absence should last at least two months, and that his departure should take place the following morning.

'That is very soon!' exclaimed Gaston.

But the Marquise kept to her resolve:

'Very well, then,' he said, 'I will start to-morrow. I merely wish to say farewell to our excellent Curé.'

'I was just going to advise you to do so. Your

departure will not surprise him, for something of the kind has already been a subject of discussion between us. The Curé has not been to see me for a long time past. He is neglecting me. Tell him so from me. Tell him also that I am hoping to see his niece from time to time when I shall be condemned once more to solitude.'

These last words were uttered in a sorrowful tone. Gaston remarked it. He was inclined to declare that he would not leave the château. But he knew his grandmother too well to be able to believe that it would be possible for him to change her determination. He therefore gave orders to his valet to prepare for their departure on the following day. Then he went to the presbytery. He had not been there since the day on which Mariette had spoken to him in the manner already related. The Curé was not at home, and the Marquis asked if he could see Mademoiselle Mariette. Johanna, in her usual bustling way, begged him to go into the parlour, and ran to tell her mistress. An instant afterwards she came back, saying, in a rather embarrassed manner, that if M. le Marquis would be good enough to wait, M. le Curé would doubtless soon be back.

'And mademoiselle,' asked Gaston, 'will she not come down?'

Johanna shrugged her shoulders, as though to say she knew nothing about it.

'Go and tell her that I beg the favour of seeing her for one moment.'

Johanna went out. She remained absent a long time, and then returned more embarrassed even than she had been on the first occasion. Mademoiselle was exceedingly sorry, but it was impossible for her to come down. If M. le Marquis would take the trouble of coming back in half an hour he would be sure to find M. le Curé at home. Gaston then wrote upon one of his visiting-cards 'To take leave,' and sent it to Mariette, begging her to receive him, as it would be impossible for him to return later on in the day. He waited with a mixture of sorrow, anxiety, and impatience the result of this last request. For the third time he saw the door of the little parlour open, and was unable to repress a gesture of satisfaction when Mariette appeared. A little paler, a little thinner than she had been at the period of their last interview, the young girl received him with composure, regretting that she had made him wait, and not appearing to remark Gaston's constrained manner when he addressed her. He was surprised and annoyed at not finding himself as much at ease as she was, or seemed to be.

'You are leaving, M. le Marquis,' she said, directing towards him her clear and innocent eyes. 'I see that you have come to bid us good-bye.'

'You are right,' said Gaston coldly; 'I am leaving

to-morrow, and it will doubtless be for a long time.'

'Madame de Saissières?' asked Mariette.

She paused. Gaston waited for the conclusion of her sentence.

'I wished to ask whether your departure does not distress Madame la Marquise very greatly?'

'O, it is she who has partly arranged it all.'

'Indeed!' said Mariette, in a slightly thoughtful tone, and as though speaking to herself; 'and yet she was so happy to have her grandson with her once more.'

'She has probably had enough of such happiness,' said Gaston.

But the next moment he reproached himself for having spoken in such a manner of his grandmother, when he knew quite well that she was making a sacrifice in depriving herself of his presence.

'What I have just said is neither right nor true,' he went on. 'If my grandmother wishes me to leave, it is only because she sees that I am not happy at home, and that she prefers my happiness to her own.'

He seemed to expect an answer—a remark from Mariette; but the young girl kept silence. The Marquis continued, pausing every now and then,

'I am only doing justice to my grandmother. I know that she is full of indulgence and kindness towards me. I wish that I could, for her sake, be something quite different from what I am. But how can I convince her that I am happy here? What more could I have done than bear the life which I lead here without complaint, and endeavour to conceal my *ennui* from her? I thought I had succeeded. It seems that I was deceiving myself. She has seen what was the matter with me. From that time my presence has given her no pleasure. I am, therefore, going to leave the château. I tell you all this, mademoiselle, because I am aware of your affection for my grandmother. May I hope that you will have the goodness, when I am no longer with her, to resume your former habit of going to see her often?'

'Certainly,' said Mariette, whose voice this time betrayed a little emotion; 'I shall be glad to think that my humble devotion may be of some service to her in her isolated, forsaken old age.'

The severe tone in which the young girl expressed herself did not escape Gaston.

'I understand you, mademoiselle,' he said: 'there is a whole world of reproaches and condemnation contained in that one sentence. You will permit me to reply to it.'

'Neither reproach nor condemnation, M. le Marquis. You ask me to go and see your grandmother. I reply that I shall be happy to do so. That is all. To whom have I reproaches to address? Whom could I allow myself to condemn?'

'Me, mademoiselle.'

'You, monsieur? Wherefore, and by what right?'

An involuntary sentiment of pride showed itself in her words.

'You seek in vain to defend yourself, mademoiselle. You blame my departure.'

'I, trying to defend myself, Monsieur le Marquis? I shall be tempted to think that you are jesting. An unfortunate and inappropriate expression of mine has doubtless furnished you with matter for raillery. Whatever it be, I think it is hardly necessary to assure you that it is impossible I should have attached to it the meaning which you have given it.'

'You think, then, that I am right in leaving?'

An expression of annoyance seemed to pass across Mariette's brow. She remained silent.

'You do not answer, mademoiselle,' persisted Gaston.

'I see that you are still jesting, monsieur.'

'Pardon me, I am not jesting, and I beg you to reply.'

'I do not know how,' answered Mariette. 'I can neither blame nor approve anything I cannot appreciate. Might I venture to beg you will have the kindness to tell Madame de Saissières that, since she wishes it, I will go and see her often?'

'You will do her good, mademoiselle, and I shall be deeply grateful to you.'

There was a moment's silence.

'I am sorry that my uncle is so late in coming back,' said Mariette. 'You wish, of course, to bid him good-bye?'

'Yes,' said Gaston absently. 'I should not like to leave without shaking hands with him. If you will permit me, I will wait; I am not at all in a hurry.'

He became once more silent. Mariette addressed some questions to him respecting the health of the marquise, to which he replied in as few words as possible. The conversation languished, and Mariette ended by being silent also, falling into a reverie which must have been very bitter, judging by the expression of her face. Gaston looked at her for some time without her being aware of it. All at once he said to her,

'We are going to separate, for who can tell how long, and shall see each other again—when? Never, perhaps. Something tells me that it ought not to be so. With regard to yourself, indeed, you lose nothing; but as for me, in leaving you—pardon the freedom with which I am speaking—I feel as though I were losing something I should never find again. We have not seen much of each other of late. For some time past, since that day when you spoke to me—do you remember it?—we have not once met. Nevertheless, this morning, when there there was a discussion between my grandmother and myself about my departure, how is it that my first thought should have been of you ?'

Mariette trembled. Raising her eyes to him,

'Why do you speak in that way ?' she said. 'You ought not to use language such as that to me. I cannot have said or done anything which entitles you to address me thus.'

'My language is the language of truth ; I tell you what I feel. If I offend you, pardon me. Permit me to say one word about myself, but one word, and only in order that you may excuse me, as I have had the misfortune to displease you. But I am displeasing you again—I see I am—by speaking in this way. I will be silent, then. Do not be too severe, Mademoiselle Mariette ; I am not entirely responsible for the foolish words which sometimes escape me. I have an unfortunate disposition. You cannot understand—you who are always so good, so reasonable—that any one can allow himself to be influenced, to be dominated, as I am. I know exactly in what respects I am deficient.'

Mariette would have been very glad to have put an end to these confidences, but Gaston continued to speak as though to himself.

'Hitherto, when I have attempted to seek and find the strength in which I am wanting, I have never succeeded in discovering anything except the power to do wrong—the power to do well, never. That which brought me back to my grandmother was not a desire to do right; it was simply weakness.'

The young girl unconsciously made a gesture of surprise—of protestation, perhaps. Then she recalled to mind the words of Madame de Saissières when passing judgment on her grandson she had said, 'He can resist nothing, and yields to everything. He is not a man; he is only a child, but one which a happy influence might convert into a superior character.'

'Forgive me, mademoiselle,' went on Gaston, 'for having spoken of myself in this way. One last word: I did not deceive myself just now, did I? You also think—you who are my grandmother's friend—that I shall do better to go away? Very well, I will do so, since you wish that I should. It is a kind of exile which you are imposing on me. Is it to last long?'

'Monsieur le Marquis,' said Mariette, surprised and embarrassed at the turn which the interview had assumed, but determined to allow nothing to take place which might seem to invest her relations towards the young man with a character they ought not to possess, 'it is doubtless on account of the kind friendship with which your grandmother honours me that you have been so good as to ask me what I think of your departure. On my side, it is in my respectful affection for Madame de Saissières that I shall perhaps be able to find some grounds for replying to your question. But when, prejudging this reply, you tell me that *I* am *imposing* an exile upon you, it becomes impossible for me to understand you, and I ask myself to whom can such expressions—which are a trifle romantic—be addressed. Not to me, certainly. They therefore dispense me from making any reply.'

Gaston bent his head, and reflected for a moment. Then, looking at Mariette, he said to her, with a gaiety, in which there was, nevertheless, a tinge of melancholy,

'You are right, mademoiselle. I was speaking in a manner which was absurd. In spite of myself, I am always overpassing the limits of reality. It is an infirmity of mine which has played me a trick more than once. Let us be serious and matter-of-fact. I am leaving to-morrow. As your uncle has not yet returned, I will give up the hope of seeing him to-day. May I venture to ask you to be good enough to tell him that, if possible, I will come very early to-morrow to shake hands with him before I start? Farewell, mademoiselle! I carry away with me, and I shall always preserve, the remembrance of what you have done for us. Allow me once more, I beg of you, to recommend my grandmother to your attention. Adieu!'

Gaston offered his hand to Mariette, who could not refuse him hers. He took that little trembling cold hand in his, held it for a moment, although she did not respond to his pressure, lifted it to his lips, and then left the room. The next moment the door of the presbytery had closed upon him. Mariette started as though the sound had hurt her; then she sat down, and remained motionless until her uncle's return. The Curé received, without making any remark, the tidings of the approaching departure of the Marquis, merely saying that he would go and bid him good-bye. Accordingly he went to the château after dinner. When he returned, he said to his niece that Madame de Saissières was not very well, and wished to see her the following day.

'We will go together to the château,' he said. 'The poor old lady will be once more alone. The Marquis will start very early in the morning, he told me, as my visit this evening dispenses him from coming here.'

And, in fact, Gaston did not return to the presbytery.

CHAPTER XIII.

'How are you to-day, my child?' asked Madame de Saissières, holding out her hand to Mariette. 'Do not tell me you are well, or I shall think that you are not speaking the truth. You are white enough to frighten any one, and from day to day your eyes get larger. You are so thin, my poor dear, that you are becoming almost transparent. Let me hear what it is that you especially suffer from to-day.'

'I do not suffer at all, madame; I am very well.'

'Your appearance and your patient resigned air give you the lie, my child. Resignation is a beautiful virtue, but upon my word you will make me detest it. It is hard for those who love you to see you suffering without your being willing to give them even the relief of a complaint. Mariette, I entreat you, pity yourself a little. Tell me that you are ill—unhappy.'

'It is a pleasure I cannot afford you, madame,' Mariette said, forcing herself to smile.

'Say, rather, that you *will* not. You are a little hypocrite. Why not speak the truth to your old friend?'

'I have nothing to tell you. I think it is cruel

of you to wish me to pity myself in order to give you pleasure.'

'Very well, darling, very well,' said the Marquise, raising her finger. 'I see what you would be at. You are trying to make a jest of it, in order that you may not be obliged to answer me. Besides, I know quite well that I shall never succeed in loosening your tongue. If, in spite of myself, I am always coming back to the charge, it is because it is terrible to see you becoming weaker and weaker every day, and losing all your colour, and yet to be constantly told that you are quite well.'

The Marquise ceased speaking. She sank into a reverie. The anxious expression of her face told of her reflections being anything but cheerful. In fact, when she suddenly roused herself from her meditation, it was in order to say to Mariette,

'I have sorrows, my darling, great sorrows.'

'If you are suffering on my account,' said Mariette, who naturally imagined that Madame de Saissières was resuming the conversation at the point at which it had been broken off, 'I entreat you not to trouble yourself any more about my health, which is really excellent.'

'On account of you, dear child!' said the Marquise, who had not heard the end of Mariette's sentence, and had already ceased to think any more of what she had just been saying. 'No, indeed. You have never caused me any grief; you have done me nothing but good. But I have received tidings of Gaston, very sad tidings.'

Mariette restrained herself from asking the question which was just about to escape her, and with her eyes fixed upon the Marquise, waited until she should explain herself. But the old lady, her chin in her hand, her brows knit, looked into vacancy, and had quite forgotten her. At last Mariette said,

'Is M. le Marquis ill, madame?'

'No,' she said, in a cold hard tone, which denoted inward irritation. 'M. le Marquis is perfectly well: But I would rather hear that he was ill of a mortal disease than know what I know.'

She said nothing more, and Mariette did not ask any further questions. At the end of a moment the Marquise passed her hand across her forehead, as though to drive away importunate thoughts, and spoke on indifferent subjects. But having by chance cast her eyes on the young girl, she suddenly said,

'Decidedly, dear child, you look worse to-day than you have hitherto done. Perhaps you are tired? Come and lie down for a moment on the sofa.'

In vain Mariette begged the Marquise to pay no attention to her; she was obliged, in order to satisfy her, to lie down and allow an antique embroidered cushion to be placed under her head.

'Now you are comfortable,' said the old lady;

'you look better already. Stay there and rest, like a good obedient child.'

She then took a little cane, which for some time past she had been wont to use to support her steps, more feeble now than they formerly were, and began to walk up and down the boudoir. Whilst she did so she continued speaking; now talking to Mariette, and now replying to her own thoughts.

'You are really unreasonable, my dear child. You are always wanting to do more than your strength will permit. Why did you come here on foot? Did I not tell you yesterday that I would send the carriage for you? My coachman has had nothing to do since Gaston left.—How long is it since my grandson went away? Months! he who did not want to go at all! I ought to have had my suspicions. When the will is so unstable, how can one count upon the heart? It was in this very room that I announced to him my intention to make him travel. "Settle my route, dear mother," he said, "and I will prove to you that if I leave you, it is only because—" Was he lying when he said that? Had he already resolved to?—Mariette, my child, why did not your uncle come to see me yesterday? Did he tell you the reason? No; at any rate, is he coming here to-day? You do not know that either? I will address very bitter reproaches to him when I next see him. At least, tell him to be certain to come to-morrow. He is surely not intending to neglect me? Do you know I cannot pardon *that?*—The route! Yes, I settled it for him, as he wished I should. He followed it for a week, and then—afterwards! Unhappy boy!—In order that this unkind Curé may not fail me to-morrow, tell him that I want to see him, Mariette. He will then be sure to come.—There are times when a wish arises in my heart to have done for ever with my ungrateful grandson, and to think no more about him. But I am old, and my end is drawing near. Can it be that my life, which was at first so brilliant and so happy, is destined to close in sorrow and isolation? It is frightful to grow old—always remain young, my child. —Gaston's silence ought to have made me guess what was happening. Besides, his last letters have been marked by a certain awkwardness and constraint; and yet he had managed to inspire me with confidence. He has the art of hiding what he feels. He is very far from suspecting that I am kept informed of everything that he does; and now he has fallen once more under the influence of that woman! He will, of course, marry her! I am told that they are travelling about together. For how long have they been doing so? I do not know exactly, and what does it signify? After such a relapse I clearly see that there is no remedy for the evil. Be it so—let him marry her. I blush that I should feel myself moved to the very depths of my soul by the thought; but enough. I have already occupied myself too much with a madman and an adventuress.—Come, Mariette, my dear child, have you nothing to say, nothing to tell me? Not one word? Well, it is I, then, who will relate to you the story of my youth. Wait a moment; I will come and sit down beside you. What! is she asleep? No! good Heavens, she has fainted!'

Yes, Mariette, lying on the sofa, had, in fact, just lost consciousness. Madame de Saissières called for assistance, and rang the bell violently; her maids hastened quickly to her, and did all they could for the young girl; but she did not come to herself until long afterwards, and not until the Marquise, in her distress, had sent off two servants on horseback to bring the Curé and the doctor. They arrived almost together, and just as Mariette was opening her eyes. The doctor said she was in a high fever, and decreed that she should at once be put to bed. But Mariette protested against anything of the kind with so much determination, and so anxiously entreated her uncle to take her home as soon as possible, that, afraid of making her worse by opposing her wishes, a carriage was hastily prepared for her. Mariette, her eyes looking brilliant from fever, her hands burning, clung to her uncle and wanted to set off immediately on foot. She was, however, put into the carriage with the Curé, and the Marquise desired the doctor to accompany them.

An hour afterwards, when he returned to the château, as Madame de Saissières had begged him to do, in order to give her tidings of his patient, he limited himself to saying, shaking his head the while,

'It is a complicated case. There is fever, congestion, nervous excitement, no reserve of strength, a weak and frail constitution. Her uncle would not believe me. A long time ago I told him that we must "tonify" her.'

CHAPTER XIV.

It is eight o'clock in the evening; the Curé and Johanna are seated opposite each other in the kitchen of the presbytery.

'Johanna,' said the Curé, in a melancholy tone, 'I forbid you to sit up again to-night. You are tired out, my poor woman. It is a fortnight since you have gone to bed. What good is it for both of us to sit up all night?'

'None, M. le Curé. That is the reason why you must go to bed.'

'It is impossible for me, Johanna.'

'And for me also, M. le Curé. I sleep very well here, beside the fire; whilst you, on the contrary, are always moving about. And it is not as if she had need of anything particular, my poor dear young lady. She lies there for hours and hours without stirring. And when one fancies that she is asleep, and goes up to her bedside, there she is lying with her poor sad eyes wide open. I tell you it cuts one to the heart. She does not seem to suffer. But we must not trust to that, for the child does not know how to complain. One might cut her into little pieces and she would still say nothing. The doctor was a little more satisfied, was he not, M. le Curé? Does he think that she will still remain for a long time to come in the state she is in now? She has no fever; I can see that quite well. When she was first taken ill she talked and laughed and cried. Now she is always gentle and quiet. If she could only eat, she would be cured. What she wants is strength.'

'Yes,' said the Curé, absorbed in sorrowful thoughts, ' yes, strength.'

At that moment a gentle knock was heard at the door of the presbytery. Johanna got up to open it; she talked for a little while with some one, and then opened the kitchen-door. A man appeared upon the threshold; after a moment's hesitation he entered. When he had removed his travelling cap, which hid a portion of his face, the Curé started as though surprised.

'You here, M. le Marquis!' he exclaimed, in a serious tone; ' I did not expect to see you.'

'I can quite understand that,' said Gaston; 'I only came back this morning.'

'Quite unexpectedly, I suppose?' inquired the Curé. ' Madame la Marquise was not expecting you, was she?'

'In point of fact, I had not announced my arrival. But, first of all, M. le Curé, give me tidings of your niece. My grandmother is very anxious about her.'

'As I have already told Madame la Marquise, my poor child continues in such a state as to give great cause for anxiety. I am even afraid she is worse. For the rest, I can add nothing to the details which Madame de Saissières has received from her doctor.'

'But I have not been made acquainted with these details. Tell me all particulars, for my own sake, if you think you need not for my grandmother's.'

The Curé remained silent, his eyes fixed on the ground.

'Is there any danger,' asked Gaston,—'any immediate danger?—Well, M. le Curé, do you not hear me?'

'I hear you, M. le Marquis. Yes, there is danger; yes, the danger is immediate. This dear and frail existence seems to be exhausted, to be evaporating, I may say, without it being possible for us to retain it.'

'And what is the cause of this strange illness?'

'If it be difficult to discover the nature of our maladies, it is much more difficult, is it not, to discover their cause?'

M. le Marquis, although surprised and hurt at the coldness displayed by the Curé, who did not even request him to sit down, patiently asked him numberless questions respecting his niece: but he only obtained evasive answers.

'I see that my presence annoys you,' he said at

last. 'Doubtless, you wish to return to Mademoiselle Mariette. Permit me to wait a moment here, and have the kindness to tell me, or to send me word, how she is.'

'I am not going to her just at present; I left her only a moment ago. Johanna is with her, and will summon me should I be wanted.'

The young man made a movement as though he were about to leave the house; then he changed his mind.

'M. le Curé,' said he, all at once, and looking at him fixedly, 'it seems to me that you do not give me the welcome which I was accustomed formerly to receive. Why is it? Is it that my grandmother has informed you of certain statements which have been made to her respecting myself? Is that the reason why you have changed in your manner towards me? Have the kindness to explain yourself frankly.'

'Allow me not to reply to your question; besides, do not forget that you are speaking to a man whose heart is bowed down with grief, and who is continually begging God to give him strength to bear the still more terrible trials with which he sees himself threatened.'

Gaston started.

'I understand you,' said he. 'But is it possible that you are almost reduced to despair? Answer me, I entreat you.'

'It would require a miracle to save her; and the too earthly feelings, which in spite of myself trouble me just now, do not allow me to hope that God will work a miracle on my behalf.'

'Grief deceives you!' exclaimed Gaston. 'It is impossible that the case should be so desperate a one. Mademoiselle Mariette is very young! Call in other doctors!'

'Doctors can do nothing more,' said the Curé, shaking his head. 'The physician who attends to the soul knows, sometimes, more than any one imagines of the state of the body. But do not let us prolong this interview, M. le Marquis. Permit me to accompany you to the door.'

Gaston withdrew in silence. When he had reached the threshold, he held out his hand to the Curé, who touched it slightly and bowed. Left alone, the poor priest endeavoured to pray for one moment before returning to his patient. Standing upright, his face hidden in his clasped hands, he strove to raise his heart and soul to God; but the bitterness of his grief scarcely allowed him to do so.

'I cannot!' he exclaimed, in a despairing tone. 'Pardon, O Lord, Thy unworthy priest, whose rebellious heart finds it impossible to bless and thank Thee for the trials which it pleases Thee to send him.'

As soon as Johanna had admitted the Marquis de Saissières into the presbytery, she went back to Mariette's room, and was surprised to see that her dear child, as she called her, had turned her face towards the door. When the old woman went up to her bedside,

'Who is there?' asked the young girl, in a low voice.

'It is I,' said Johanna, coming close to her.

'No; down-stairs—with my uncle. I heard some one talking.'

'O, it is M. le Marquis, mademoiselle. He is come to inquire after you.'

Something like a ray of renewed life passed over Mariette's colourless face; after which she became even paler than before, closed her eyes, and remained silent. Johanna thought that she was going to sleep, and sat down quietly near her bedside. When, after the departure of M. de Saissières, the Curé gently opened the door of the room, Johanna put her finger to her lips as a sign to him to keep silence. But Mariette, opening her eyes, said,

'It is you, uncle? I want to speak to you. Come in. Leave us, my good Johanna.'

Johanna, at once surprised and bewildered at seeing that her young mistress suddenly seemed much better, hastened to withdraw.

The interview between uncle and niece was a long one. When at last the Curé recalled Johanna, she found her setting up in bed, and the Curé standing before her in an attitude of meditation.

'It shall be as you wish, my child,' he said, in a grave and sorrowful tone. 'I think—indeed, I even feel—that I *ought* to grant your request. God has His own means, which are known to Him alone, for bringing back an unhappy man who is fleeing from Him. It would be impossible for Him to make use of a hand which is more innocent than yours. Act, then, according to the inspiration which He sends you. Only take care that no earthly sentiment unconsciously mingles itself with the pure impulse of charity to which I authorise you to yield.'

'Do not be afraid of anything, uncle,' answered Mariette, with gentle firmness. 'I can without presumption assure you that I am certain of myself. If I be destined, as I believe I am, to carry out a good work, I shall be happy to employ the remnant of strength which remains to me in performing it.'

The Curé looked at her with anguish whilst she thus spoke.

'You shall see him, then,' said he. 'And now, child, lie down again and sleep, if it be possible.'

The next day, when the doctor went to the presbytery, he was told that his patient wanted to leave her bed. He shrugged his shoulders.

'She has not strength enough,' he said. But after after having seen her, he said to her uncle, 'Let her try. It is an invalid's fancy. There is no use in opposing her; it would only be productive of harm.

I still believe, however, that she will find she is not able to rise.'

Aided by Johanna, Mariette got up and dressed herself, putting on the little cotton dress she had always worn, and which was now far too large for her emaciated form. When she had recovered breath, after making this great effort, she said to Johanna,

'I want to go down-stairs.'

The faithful servant exclaimed, raised her arms heavenwards, and ran to fetch her master.

The Curé, after having refused, ended by yielding to the persuasions and entreaties of his niece, feeling at once happy and almost alarmed at seeing her out of bed. So she was wrapped up well, placed in an armchair, and carried gently down-stairs. Then she asked to be taken to the parlour.

'You wish to see him this very day, do you?' asked the Curé sorrowfully.

'Yes,' said she. 'How can I tell? I have not, perhaps, much time to lose.'

Soon afterwards a slight knock at the front door made her tremble.

'It is M. de Saissières,' said she. 'Uncle, bring him in here.

'Yes, but not before I have said one word to him.' And he went and opened the door for the Marquis.

'Permit me to receive you here,' said he, leading

Gaston into the kitchen. 'The parlour is not at liberty. I wish to speak to you.'

As soon as he was alone with the young man he crossed his arms on his breast, and fixed his penetrating and sombre eyes upon him.

'If there be anything,' he said at last, in a deep voice, 'which can produce a durable impression upon a frivolous and vacillating character such as yours, it will be what you are going to hear to-day, M. le Marquis.'

'Speak, M. le Curé, I am listening,' said Gaston.

'I have very little to tell you. The serious words to which you are about to listen will proceed from another mouth, from a mouth which death is about to close.'

The Curé bent his head and seemed to be endeavouring to preserve composure; then he raised it again, and drawing himself up to the full height of his tall figure,

'Monsieur le Marquis,' he said, fixing once more a piercing gaze upon him, 'my niece wishes to speak to you. She believes that you will listen to the warnings and counsels she is about to give you with her dying voice. I know and approve the reasons springing from—from Christian charity, which led her to desire this interview. Yes, I approve of them. As to yourself, young man, if you should be unfortunate enough not to understand them'—here he seized him involuntarily by the arm and held it in his strong grasp,—'if you should be mad enough to misunderstand her, to forget for one single moment that you are in the presence of an angel, who in her goodness casts a glance of pity upon a miserable sinner, I will drive you hence at once; yes, I will drive you hence. I am a priest, monsieur, but I am also a man! Take care!'

His eyes darted forth flames; an inexplicable emotion caused the veins of his forehead to swell. Suddenly he loosened his hold of the Marquis's arm, and stepped back shaking his head; then in a low voice and in a tone which was full of sorrow and humility,

'May God have pity on me!' he exclaimed. 'I suffer, M. le Marquis. Forget the way in which I have just spoken; I have given way, I am afraid, to feelings which are forbidden me by the habit I wear. But I am no longer a man; I am only a priest! Come, monsieur, my niece is waiting for you.'

And without leaving Gaston time to recover from the surprise and emotion which this strange scene had occasioned him, he led him towards the parlour and knocked gently at the door. Seeing that his niece, who was perfectly calm, had slowly turned her face, illuminated by a sweet serenity, towards them, he desired the Marquis to enter, and left them alone together, as soon as he had assured himself that his beloved patient was comfortably supported by the cushions which Johanna had placed in her easy-chair.

He then withdrew to his chamber, where he prayed and shed tears, which are sometimes perhaps but another way of praying. At the end of half an hour, as he was about to enter the parlour, the door opened, and Gaston came out. He bowed silently to the Curé, and at once left the presbytery.

'Thanks,' said Mariette, extending her hand to her uncle as soon as she saw him make his appearance. 'I have finished the work I wanted to do.'

The Curé cast an anxious look at the pale face, from which there beamed at this moment a ray of pure and sweet satisfaction.

'I am well,' murmured the young girl, in answer to the mute inquiry addressed to her; 'only a little tired.'

She was, in fact, so exhausted that she allowed herself to be carried to her bed without making any remonstrance, and, almost immediately afterwards, fell into a profound sleep.

Days passed, and Mariette remained in the same state; she seemed happy, but her strength did not return. Every morning Gaston came to the presbytery, asked very particularly after her, and then withdrew. His interviews with the Curé were always very short. Some few words which escaped from him proved that he constantly saw the doctor who was attending Mariette, and that he received from him all particulars respecting her state. As to the conversation which he had had with the Curé's niece, he never made the slightest allusion to it.

One evening Mariette felt herself much worse; her habitual serenity having been succeeded by great nervous agitation, followed by high fever. The doctor was summoned; and, on leaving the patient's room, he said to the Curé, who scarcely dared to question him,

'I hope that we shall get over this crisis. But if another should supervene—'

'And is it likely that a fresh attack may soon come on?'

'To-morrow, perhaps; but I will not leave you until the present seizure has passed over. I will await the effect of the remedies which I have administered. Go to your niece, and call me as soon as any change takes place.'

An hour afterwards, the Curé, to his great relief, seeing that Mariette had fallen asleep, went downstairs. He there found the Marquis de Saissières with the doctor. In his preoccupation, he did not think of being astonished at his presence.

'Come, doctor, come quickly,' he said. 'I fancy there is a change.'

When they came back, M. de Saissières questioned the doctor in a trembling voice.

'The crisis has passed over. But I have warned M. le Curé that if another supervenes the worst is to be feared.'

'And do you think that it will?'

'I think it probable. We will, however, do all in our power to prevent it.'

And as he left the presbytery with Gaston, he said to him,

'She is lost! The fever will return to-morrow, or the day after, and we shall not be able to subdue it.'

CHAPTER XV.

THE next day the Marquis went early in the morning to the presbytery, and asked to speak to the Curé, who received him at once, telling him that Mariette had passed a good night, but that his anxiety was not thereby diminished. Gaston listened to him in silence. He was pale, and bore on his face the traces of a sleepless night.

'M. le Curé,' he said all at once, and in a very serious tone, 'I am going to ask you a strange question. Has mademoiselle, your niece, never requested to see me?'

'No,' answered the Curé, looking at him with surprise.

'And has she never spoken of me?'

'Why these questions, M. le Marquis?'

'You know the reason, M. le Curé; have the goodness to answer me.'

'I think,' said the Curé, hesitating, 'that my niece has asked once or twice after Madame de Saissières, and after you also, monsieur.'

'May I be informed in what terms she expressed herself?'

'She merely inquired if you were still at the château.'

'And is she aware that I have come here every day?'

'No, monsieur.'

'Well, M. le Curé,' said Gaston slowly, 'I entreat you to tell mademoiselle, your niece, that I beg she will do me the honour to receive me as soon as she is well enough.'

The Curé shook his head.

'You refuse to grant my request?'

'It needs no answer. You do not seem to understand the nature of the case, young man. We do not speak of visits to a dying person.'

'Mademoiselle, your niece, is not dying,' said the young Marquis energetically; 'but she is threatened with imminent peril. Her illness may become mortal at any moment; I know what her state is better than you imagine. May I hope that you will have the kindness to transmit my request to Mademoiselle Marie du Reux?'

'No, Monsieur le Marquis,' replied the Curé, repressing, with difficulty, the impatience he felt. 'Do not say any more about it, I beg.'

'M. le Curé, I conjure you not to persist in your refusal!'

'And I, M. le Marquis, beg you to withdraw. My niece is not in a state to receive you.'

'Allow her to decide that question herself.'

'No, monsieur.'

'You shall be present at our interview, if my request be granted.'

'Tell me what you wish to say to my niece; I shall then be able to judge whether there be anything in it which I can repeat to her.'

'In the name of Heaven, M. le Curé, do not be hindered by what may seem to be an extraordinary request on my part, but deign to grant it. Since I appeal to mademoiselle herself to decide whether she will see me or not, what is there for you to fear? O, is it possible that you still hesitate?'

'Well, then, be it so, monsieur. I consent that my niece should be made aware that you have expressed a wish to see her.'

'You will tell her?'

'Yes.'

'When?'

'When I have a convenient opportunity.'

'I entreat you do not delay. Is she asleep just now?'

'I do not think so.'

'Go to her, then, M. le Curé. I will await her answer here.'

'What, monsieur!' exclaimed the Curé, with an irritation he could no longer master. 'You surely cannot imagine that it will be possible for my niece to receive you to-day?'

'I do not imagine anything. I await her commands.'

The Curé shook his head.

'Do not wait,' he said. 'I promise to transmit your request to my niece. Come here to-morrow for the answer.'

'I will return in a short time,' said the Marquis, retiring.

Soon afterwards the Curé, finding that his niece was better than she had been for several days past, thought that he might fulfil the promise he had made to Gaston. His upright simple character was unacquainted with the art of making preliminary speeches.

'My child,' said he, 'M. de Saissières came here, a little while ago, to inquire after you. When he found that you were better, he begged me to tell you that he wished to see you as soon as it was possible for you to receive him.'

Mariette, without answering, closed her eyes and remained motionless for a moment; an imperceptible movement of her lips seemed to give evidence that she was praying.

'You have brought me very happy tidings, uncle, although you have no idea of it yourself.'

'May I be allowed to know what they are?'

'Certainly. I am ready to explain myself. When I fell ill at the château, Madame de Saissières had just received news respecting her grandson which grieved her deeply. She was telling me about it when I lost consciousness. It was doubtless on that account that, during the fever which afterwards attacked me, I was constantly occupying myself with Madame de Saissières and her grandson; and it was also then that I had a strange kind of dream. I beheld the Marquis de Saissières suspended over a frightful abyss. Some little bushes to which he was clinging broke in his hands. Near him stood his grandmother, powerless to aid him. Stretching out his arms he called on me for help. I felt that I was possessed of the power of saving the Marquis. I stretched out my hands to him, he seized them, regained the edge of the precipice, and without thinking of me rushed into the arms of his grandmother, who offered me her thanks. The next moment I flew away. Do you never dream that you are flying? It is such a delightful sensation. Unfortunately it was the end of my dream. I awoke directly afterwards. But falling asleep again, I recommenced my dream, and seemed to be for ever beholding the same scene. It tired me to death, when at last, the fever having left me, I became once more myself; but my dream was converted into a fixed idea, and I felt as though it really depended upon me to save the Marquis from a still greater danger, and to restore happiness to his grandmother. I repulsed the notion as much as I could; but, by little and little, it took firm possession of my mind. What else have I now to add, my uncle, my father, but that, after having heard my confession, you authorised me to see the Marquis. I spoke to him in the words with which Heaven inspired me, and I prayed that what I had said might produce the effect I so ardently desired. The message you have just brought makes me hope that my prayer has been heard. I must see M. de Saissières once more and for the last time, if you will permit me.'

'I permit you,' said the Curé, hesitating. 'But you must begin by gaining a little strength. In order to do so, you must take very great care of yourself. When you are quite well, we will go to the château, and there—'

'But, uncle, I must see M. de Saissières this very day.'

'To-day, Mariette! You cannot be in earnest, surely.'

'Pardon me, uncle, I am, and you must permit me. Have the kindness to send Johanna here. I must get up, and I will see M. de Saissières as soon as he returns here.'

'I cannot permit anything of the kind,' said the Curé.

The arrival of the doctor put an end to their conversation, and Mariette asked him to allow her to rise. The Curé protested, but the doctor stopped him.

'It will, perhaps, be as well she should,' he said, in a low voice. 'Let her do as she likes.'

When Gaston came back, the Curé said to him with a sigh, and without even waiting for a question,

'My niece will receive you, M. le Marquis. I will take you to her. But,' he added, with sorrowful resignation, 'you will not forget that she has, doubtless, only a very short time to live, and you will see that she does not try her strength overmuch. Do not stay long with her.'

So saying, he made him mount a steep and narrow staircase and led him into a closet, which served as an anteroom to the bedchamber of the young girl, who was too weak now to be taken downstairs. Mariette was seated in an easy-chair, looking so white that she might have been taken for a waxen figure. Gaston was touched, and was obliged to pause for a moment upon the threshold, until Mariette welcomed him with a look, and invited him to take a seat opposite to her. He sat down in silence, but seeing that the Curé was about to withdraw,

'Stay here,' he said. 'It costs me nothing to speak before you.'

'Stay, I beg of you, uncle,' said Mariette. 'It was not for me to ask you to do so; but since M. le Marquis has no objection—'

'No, my child,' answered the Curé; 'I will remain within call, and if you want me you can summon me. M. le Marquis, do not forget that it is a convalescent who is receiving you.'

The manner in which he said 'convalescent' gave to the word an entirely different signification from the one it usually bears.

He withdrew.

Gaston looked at Mariette in silence.

'Well,' she said, rather impatiently as it were, 'what is it you have to say to me?'

'Do you not know? Did I not tell you that I would not come back until your commands had been executed? They have been.'

'Really!' said she, in a glad and gentle tone..

'All is at an end, and at an end for ever,' said Gaston. 'I wrote—'

Mariette stopped him by a gesture.

'You remember,' said she, 'that I will not and ought not to know anything.'

'That is true. But will you be so kind as to read this letter.'

'What is it?' asked Mariette, hesitating, whilst taking in her hand the letter offered to her by Gaston.

'It is from my grandmother, and is addressed to you.'

Mariette read as follows:

'My dear Child,—Thanks! You have given my son back to me. God has made use of you in order

to work a miracle. It only needed a few words from
your mouth, my dear little saint, to rekindle right
sentiments in his benumbed heart. Gaston, after
having seen you, came in search of me, and spoke to
me in terms such as I have never hitherto heard him
utter. I listened without being able to believe him.
But words were followed by deeds. There are some
things of which we cannot speak to a child, pure as
you are. I almost regret it. I should like you to be
able to comprehend how much courage was required
by this convert of yesterday to break through the
meshes in which he had once more become entangled.
Let it suffice you to know that he is saved; and I,
giving vent once more to sweet tears, such as I have
for a long time past been a stranger to, have been able
to open to him my arms and say, "Behold the son of
my son!" My first tribute of gratitude is due to you.
God has the second only. It is not right, perhaps;
but it is so. My dear child, I bless you. How I
long to press you also to my heart! But, like you, I am
ill. Live to be still our angel guardian, our blessing,
and our joy!   MARQUISE DE SAISSIÈRES.'

Whilst reading these lines, Mariette, although
always able to exercise self-control, changed colour
several times. The blood mounted from time to time
to her cheeks, only to leave them paler afterwards
than they had been before. When she had finished,

she unconsciously allowed the letter to slip out of her fingers, and covering her face with her hands, she wept silently. Gaston, as pale as herself, came and knelt down beside her easy-chair, taking one of her hands in his and finally retaining it. Then he said to her, in so low and agitated a voice as to be barely intelligible,

'Will you allow me to speak to you, now, a little about yourself?'

'No,' said Mariette, disengaging her hand, and hastily drying her tears. 'My name must not even be pronounced. Speak to me about your grandmother; tell me that you are happy, like her, and thank God.'

Gaston put his head close to the head of the young girl, and whispered,

'Marie, do you love me?'

A crimson flush suffused the cheeks of the Curé's niece, who, suddenly regaining strength, rose to her feet. Fixing upon the young man a gaze in which fear, shame, indignation, alternately showed themselves,

'What have I done? What have I done to merit such an outrage?' she exclaimed, in a hurried tone.

Gaston, still on his knees and raising his hands with an entreating gesture, exclaimed,

'Marie, I love you! Will you be my wife?'

The young girl stretched out her arms, uttered a

piercing cry, then, stiff and inanimate, she fell upon the floor.

The door opened instantly, the Curé entered, and hastening to his niece, he took her in his arms.

'Unhappy man,' he exclaimed, in a heart-rending voice, turning towards Gaston, 'you have killed her!'

CHAPTER XVI.

DAY was about to dawn, and Gaston was alone in the parlour at the presbytery. Leaning on the table, his forehead hid in his hands, he seemed overwhelmed by despair, and a prey to some horrible anxiety. Frequently raising his head, he listened, but hearing nothing, again hid his face. At last the sound of steps was heard approaching, and the Curé appeared at the door.

'Well?' asked the young man, starting to his feet and speaking in a scarcely audible tone.

The priest did not reply. He leant for a moment against the wall, as if he had not strength to stand; then he let himself fall upon a chair, uttering a profound sigh.

'In the name of Heaven, speak!' exclaimed the Marquis, stretching out his hand towards him.

'She lives; she has recognised us,' said the old man, in a quivering voice.

Making a violent effort, and recovering a little composure,

'Pardon me,' he continued; 'my emotion has overcome me for a moment; I ought to have remembered that my tardiness in answering you was prolonging your suspense. But I was unable to speak. Thanks be to God, my niece lives! Without as yet being able to pronounce any definite opinion with regard to the consequences of this terrible seizure, the doctor assures us that there is no immediate danger to be feared.'

Then, allowing time to the young man in his turn to recover from his too visible emotion, the Curé invited him by a gesture to sit down.

'Now that we are again restored to momentary tranquillity,' he said, 'you will understand, M. le Marquis, that I await an account of what has taken place between my niece and yourself. It is an explanation that must not be deferred. Speak then.'

'I will give it you without hesitation or evasion, M. le Curé. Must I begin by telling you what was the subject of the first interview which Mademoiselle du Reux was so good as to grant me?'

'It is useless, monsieur. I am acquainted with all that I need know about it.'

'There remains, then, but little for me to tell you. However much I might wish it, I should never be able to explain the change which took place in me after that conversation. For the first time in my life, I knew what it was to blush for myself. I felt at last, to its full extent and in all its power, the wholesome shame with which my grandmother and you had so often sought in vain to inspire me; and I found in it a strength which I had never known before. What more can I say? And now I have broken definitely with the past. It does not exist any longer for me. I am free. My grandmother is happy, and I have placed in the hands of Mademoiselle du Reux a letter in which her old friend thanks her, blesses her, and calls her at once her good angel and her child.'

'Well, monsieur,' said the Curé coldly, 'it gives me pleasure to hear that God has restored you to yourself. I abstain from remarking that once before this miracle seemed to have been worked upon you; that then also—it is not so long ago—you said that you had freed yourself for ever.'

'No, M. le Curé,' exclaimed Gaston impetuously, 'I was not then—'

'Stop, monsieur,' interrupted the priest, in a serious tone; 'I do not mean to say more on that subject. To come back to my niece: it was the reading, then, of the letter of Madame de Saissières—'

'I have not yet told you all,' continued Gaston earnestly. 'I have offered to Mademoiselle du Reux, not only the expression of my grandmother's gratitude, but also, M. le Curé, the homage of an unlimited affection, and the ardent supplication of a man who has dared, all unworthy though he be of her, to beg her to accept his name.'

The Curé rose abruptly and stepped backwards.

His surprise was such that he seemed to seek in vain for words in which to express it.

'What does this language signify, monsieur?' he cried at last, fixing upon the young man an angry look.

'It does not appear to me that it is very difficult to catch the meaning of my words, M. le Curé.'

'Monsieur,' said the priest, with profound stupefaction, 'I cannot believe for one moment that you are jesting; I am therefore induced to imagine that you are dreaming, or that I am dreaming myself.'

'And why?' said Gaston. 'Why? A jest or dream do you call it? No, monsieur. No. My words are the exact and sincere expression of my truest sentiments, of my dearest wishes. I love Mademoiselle du Reux, and I have asked her to become my wife.'

'M. le Marquis,' exclaimed the Curé, in a severe tone, 'if some new fancy is taking possession of your mind, could I have expected that my niece, who is ill of a mortal complaint, was destined to be the object of it? Shall I be obliged to ask you to leave my house and never to set foot in it again? By addressing this saint in the language which it appears you have held towards her, you have committed an act which is exceedingly disloyal in the eyes of the world, and highly culpable in the sight of God.'

'Circumstances sometimes authorise actions which

the world condemns, but to which God gives absolution.'

'Really, young man, you are, it seems, very sure of yourself and of God also. But no more of this. I will confine myself to telling you that you have entirely failed in your duty towards me, and even towards her to whom your insane homage is addressed.'

Gaston shook his head.

'I have not failed in my duty towards Mademoiselle du Reux. I appeal to herself, and I will have no other judge in this matter. As to you, M. le Curé, if I did not first demand your consent, it was because I felt that I was certain to meet with invincible opposition on your part, and that I was irrevocably resolved not to yield to it. Warned of what I had determined to say to Mademoiselle du Reux, you would have prevented me from seeing her. I begged you to be present at our interview. It was you who would not remain.'

'Stop, monsieur; you are speaking clearly and resolutely. Do you dare to say that my niece's conduct towards you can, even for one moment, have authorised you to address her in the extravagant terms you have done?'

'No, M. le Curé. Her conduct, which has always been full of reserve and dignity, would, on the contrary, have rather tended to deprive me of the courage of telling her that I loved her. And yet—'

Gaston hesitated.

'Go on, monsieur,' said the Curé, darting towards him a fiery glance.

'And yet,' continued the young man calmly, 'I believed that I was authorised in speaking to her. It remains for me to tell you that I acquainted my grandmother with my sentiments, my intentions, and my resolution to have an interview this very day with Mademoiselle du Reux.'

'And Madame la Marquise consented?' exclaimed the Curé, overwhelmed with astonishment. 'Monsieur, monsieur, it is not possible!'

'Observe that I did not exactly ask her consent. I simply acquainted her with my sentiments, and my determination, over which neither time nor obstacles, should any present themselves, will be able to exercise any influence.'

'And it was after receiving your communication that Madame de Saissières wrote my niece the letter of which you have just spoken?'

'The letter was already written, and in my hands, when I explained myself to her. And, after all, it signified but little, as the letter contained only the just expression of my grandmother's feelings towards mademoiselle, your niece.'

'You wish, then, monsieur, to give me to understand that Madame de Saissières approves your projects, your dreams, with regard to my niece?'

Gaston merely replied that he had no opposition to fear on her side.

The Curé smiled bitterly, and seemed about to make an angry reply. But he restrained himself, and simply said,

'Would you think it right to acquaint me with my niece's answer? If not, I will apply to her for it.'

'Mademoiselle du Reux did not make me any answer. I had hardly finished speaking when she lost consciousness, and you came in.'

'Very well, M. le Marquis. I think it useless to prolong our interview.'

'But my answer? You will speak to mademoiselle, your niece, will you not, M. le Curé? If, as I believe, there is good reason to hope she will deign to accept—'

'Come, M. le Marquis,' interrupted the Curé, with a mixture of anger and grief, 'put an end to this romantic language, which is all the more insane because the subject of it is a young girl whose days are already numbered.'

'Mademoiselle du Reux will live!' cried Gaston, in a ringing voice. 'She will live, and she will be my wife, because—why should I be afraid to tell you? —because she loves me! A thousand signs have shown it me; and I have now only one desire, only one ambition, that of consecrating my life to her happiness!'

The Curé seemed at first as though he wished to make a vehement protestation; then he struck his forehead.

'O youth! O folly!' he exclaimed. 'M. le Marquis, come back to yourself, and speak in terms such as are more worthy of you. If what you suppose be true, in the name of Heaven, have pity on a poor girl from whom everything separates you; and instead of speaking of consecrating your life to her, leave her, and never see her again.'

'And wherefore, M. le Curé? I cannot believe you will persist in refusing my alliance.'

'And what do I care for the honour of an alliance which would make the unhappiness of my niece? Do not protest. I know what you are going to say. But your vows and your transports, what are they all worth? And how culpable am I for the want of foresight which has paved the way for all these misfortunes! You wish to snatch my niece away from a humble and modest life—a life of sacrifice, I grant, but a life which leads her to God—in order to offer her—what? Sufferings without compensation—sufferings which always follow upon disproportionate marriages. Never, monsieur, never!'

'Have confidence in me, M. le Curé,' said Gaston, with persuasive gentleness.

'Alas,' exclaimed the Curé bitterly, 'it is, perhaps, on the edge of a grave that we are speaking thus! But what does it matter? I will do my duty. I will repair the evil I have caused. I will speak to your grandmother. I will speak to my niece. God will inspire me.'

And he dismissed Gaston without allowing him to utter another word.

CHAPTER XVII.

MARIETTE, convalescent now, was listening with feelings of happiness, mingled with doubt, to Gaston, who was seated by her side, almost at her feet, and who was speaking to her of love. What did he say to her? Just what we have all of us said so often, with so much confidence in feelings which seemed as though they would endure for ever, and which lasted so short a time. Projects for the future, which were almost childish in their character, succeeded by tender vows.

Mariette had not yet been able to go out. On her side, the Marquise, who was still suffering, was confined to her easy-chair, so that they had not yet met. But Gaston asserted that Madame de Saissières was ardently longing to see her future granddaughter, and to clasp her in her arms. The Curé had had an interview with the Marquise; and after a long conversation with Mariette, he had appeared to feel that he might give Gaston permission to come and see his niece from time to time.

'I leave you mistress of your fate,' said he to her. 'I can do nothing more now, excepting pray for you.'

Mariette, agitated and uneasy, dared not trust to Gaston's protestations, and asked question after question respecting Madame de Saissières' real feelings towards her. In spite of her doubts, the happiness of being loved gave her renewed life, and her strength was returning so fast, that in a little while she was certain she would be able to go to the château.

The lovers had been talking together for a long while, when the Curé came to tell Gaston that it was time for him to take his leave. Things usually passed in this manner, for the Marquis was a little apt to forget himself. Grief and anxiety had traced their lines upon the face of the aged Curé. After the young man had left, he remained a moment with his niece, and inquired particularly after her health, appearing as happy as was possible for him to be now, at seeing her gradually recovering vitality. Then he retired, and soon afterwards his niece heard him go out. The young girl seemed lost in thought. Her face, which had at first been serious, was soon illuminated by a smile. Evidently her day-dream was a happy one. But Johanna disturbed it. Looking frightened, she told her young mistress that a lady desired to speak to her.

'A lady!' exclaimed Mariette. 'Who is it? Good Heavens, can it be the Marquise?'

No, it was a lady whom Johanna had never seen, and who did not belong to the neighbourhood—a beautiful lady.

'What can she want with me?'

Johanna could not tell.

'Go and ask her, Johanna. She wishes to see me, I suppose, about some charitable object. If it be so, it will be better she should speak to my uncle.'

Johanna came back with a note written upon a page torn out of a memorandum-book:

'If you remember the person whose protection you claimed on a certain evening, when you were detained against your will in M. Gaston de Saissières' apartment, grant her a few moments' conversation. You will thereby render a service to him whom you love, and will save him from peril.'

The words, 'him whom you love,' made Mariette's cheeks flush. How could this woman speak so freely of feelings which Mariette shrank from confessing even to herself? How was it possible that this creature, for whom Madame de Saissières felt nothing but contempt, and by whom Gaston had been nearly ruined, could speak of such love as Mariette's without profaning it? The Curé's niece wished at first to refuse the request which had been made to her for an interview. She had already put the note into an envelope, and had desired Johanna to give it back to the lady, and to tell her that she could not receive her, when the thought of danger menacing Gaston suddenly struck her. Supposing it were true? Mariette would have liked to consult her uncle. She desired Johanna to ask the lady whether she would be good enough to wait. But she sent word back that she could not, and that she would go away never to return, if Mariette did not at once receive her. The young girl hesitated no longer.

'Tell the lady that I am coming down.'

And the next moment she entered the room where the stranger was awaiting her.

The two women bowed to each other in silence. Then the visitor examined Mariette attentively, whilst the Curé's niece, inviting her by a gesture to be seated, said briefly,

'You wished to see me, madame. I await the communication which you desire to make.'

'Yes,' she slowly answered, 'the communication relative to Gaston, is it not? I thought that would be sure to interest you.'

On hearing his name proceed from those lips, Mariette involuntarily drew herself up.

'Is it not true,' inquired the other, with a sorrowful smile,—' is it not true that if I had not invoked Gaston's name I should not have been admitted into your presence? Do not blush, young girl.'

Mariette, indeed, felt she was blushing, but that it was from annoyance rather than from confusion.

'I am waiting, madame, until you shall be pleased to explain yourself,' she said calmly.

She held in her hand the note which the stranger had just written to her.

'Yes, yes, I know,' she said, in a languid manner. 'I have spoken to you of a danger which menaces *him*. Good Heavens, how shall I express myself! It is certain that if Gaston were to fall into the hands of my brother he would not show him much mercy. But he is a long way off at present. He has, in fact, expatriated himself. It is hardly likely he will come from America in order to revenge himself. So you may be quite easy in that respect. As for me, I have many reasons for being angry with Gaston; but I am not vindictive. I forgive him his quite involuntary treason—such treasons always are involuntary. You have therefore nothing to fear, on my side, for my faithless lover, in connection with me.'

The careless assurance with which this had been said rendered the language in which it was couched all the more insupportable to Mariette. She made a gesture, as though about to rise from her chair, saying,

'The object of this conversation escapes me, madame.'

'To tell the truth,' said the stranger, with a faint smile, 'I wanted to speak to you, not of a danger which was menacing Gaston, but of one to which you are yourself exposed in giving your heart to so faithless a man, and in allowing yourself to be seduced by his protestations of love.'

Mariette trembled and rose, her face suffused with blushes.

'Alas, yes,' pursued the stranger, ' your fate, my beautiful child, will be the same as mine, and the same as that of many others who have preceded you in the affections of too frivolous a heart, and one always open to new impressions. In common with us all, you flatter yourself, my dear little girl, that you will be able to fix his heart. It is an error. Gaston will soon be tired of you, and then he will forsake you, just as he has forsaken many others also. I tell you all this because I really pity you. Your inexperience renders the combat between such a lover and yourself too unequal.'

Carried away by a movement of indignation, Mariette said, in a trembling voice,

'You are ignorant, madame, that it is to the future Marquise Gaston de Saissières that you are speaking thus.'

It was the turn of the lady to start.

'What are you saying?' she exclaimed. 'What, the haughty Marquis de Saissières! For these people imbibe pride with the milk that nourishes them, and Gaston is at the bottom of his heart as vain as his equals. Is it possible, then, that the Marquis has really spoken of giving his noble name, his title, his coat of arms, to the niece of the Curé?'

'Who, noble herself, will quarter her arms with those of her husband!' exclaimed Mariette.

These words, which she regretted the moment after they were spoken, had been torn from her by an irresistible feeling of wounded pride. She had been trained by her father to respect the name she bore, and taught that, although she did not possess a title of nobility, her rank was not on that account lower or less ancient. She had made a sacrifice of all her weaknesses to her uncle; but this one still survived, perhaps unconsciously to herself.

'Really,' exclaimed the lady, looking at Mariette with a kind of mocking curiosity, 'we have already got to that! Whatever may be your rank, my child, you will allow me to believe that, in Gaston's eyes, your coat of arms is your pretty face. But do not be angry. I have no intention of offending you. I only fear that in your ingenuous confidence you will allow yourself to become a prey to great illusions as regards the intentions of the Marquis. In any case you cannot forget his grandmother; and I forewarn you that she is inflexible in the matter of love-matches. Has she any suspicion of what has taken place between Gaston and you?'

'Madame la Marquise de Saissières has given her consent to our marriage,' said Mariette, with trembling lips.

She felt that it would have been more worthy of her not to have replied to such a question. But she yielded, spite of herself, to the influence of the woman who was questioning her with so much calmness and assurance.

Speaking deliberately, the stranger said,

'If it be so, I can but congratulate you upon your happy future. Will you allow me, however, to give you one piece of advice? Hasten your marriage, and become Madame la Marquise as soon as possible. Do not rely upon the promises of the Marquis, however tenderly you may love him, and however much you may imagine yourself to be beloved. This disinterested advice will prove to you that I do not entertain the faintest hope of being able to separate you from Gaston. I am acting with the most complete disinterestedness. I do not love the young man— the boy, I ought to say—any longer. My brother wished to force him to marry me; but, for my own part, I have never had any ambitious views. If I came here to see you, it was only through curiosity; and because I had a fancy to look at the person for whom my faithless lover had forsaken me. I hardly saw you the first time we met, and I must confess that the remembrance I had of you did not entirely serve to explain Gaston's conduct. Now, however, I see you really are lovely, very lovely, and I am better pleased it should be so. Perhaps you do possess all that is required in order to hold empire over Gaston, and retain it. I hope it may be so for your sake, since you are about to become, so it appears, his wife.

And now farewell. Accept my best wishes for your happiness.'

Whilst thus speaking, the stranger had risen, and offered Mariette the tips of her elegantly-gloved fingers. It would have been impossible for the young girl to touch her hand; she therefore bowed in silence. The visitor gave an indifferent smile, and, bowing slightly, left the room with careless grace.

Mariette was greatly agitated by this visit, and spoke of it to her uncle, who listened to her with bent brows, confining himself, however, to advising her not to say anything about it to Gaston for the present. It was not without repugnance Mariette submitted to his advice. Sorrow, mingled with uneasiness, weighed upon her heart, and poisoned days which ought to have brought her nothing but joy and happiness. The hours which she spent with Gaston were, perhaps, only all the sweeter because then she forgot everything. Nevertheless she longed to see the Marquise as soon as possible. In vain she endeavoured to make her uncle tell her what had passed between the aged lady and himself; he made her only laconic replies.

'She has given her consent, and it was only in consequence of her wishes that I permitted her grandson to return here. As to the rest, you will speak to her yourself.'

As soon as Mariette was strong enough, she asked to be taken to the château. A carriage belonging to

Gaston was sent to convey her and her uncle there. The Marquis received them at the entrance. He gave his arm to his *fiancée*, and took her to his grandmother. Mariette felt as though she should die. She was obliged to pause for a moment before entering the apartments of the Marquise; but a look full of tenderness which Gaston cast upon her gave her a little strength. When they entered her boudoir, Madame de Saissières, unable to leave her easy-chair, endeavoured, nevertheless, to sit upright, and then watched them coming towards her. Her sorrowful gaze was fixed more especially on Mariette, who instinctively attempted to withdraw the hand which she was leaning upon Gaston's arm, but he prevented her. As soon as they were standing in front of her easy-chair,

'Mother,' said he, 'I bring you my *fiancée*, your daughter—open to her your arms.'

The Marquise remained mute and motionless, still directing the same cold and mournful gaze upon the Curé's niece. There was a moment's painful silence. All at once, Mariette, quitting Gaston's arm, sank down almost to Madame de Saissières' feet. The old lady slowly raised her wrinkled hand, and laid it upon the young girl's head.

'Marie du Reux,' she said, with a mixture of affection and reproach, 'is it thus that we are destined to meet once more? My son, do not interrupt me; let me speak, or else take away your *fiancée*.'

'Mother,' exclaimed the Marquis, 'this is not what you promised me!'

'And what was it I promised you, my son? Not to oppose your marriage. Do not be afraid; I will be faithful to my promise. As to the rest, what is it you expect from me? That I should say I am happy, when I am not? It would be asking too much. Must I be silent? Be it so. I can be silent. But in that case you must leave me.'

'No, no!' exclaimed Mariette, distracted. 'Speak, speak!'

Gaston was about to impose silence on his grandmother, when the Curé came forward.

'M. le Marquis,' he said, 'I wish my niece to speak freely with madame, your grandmother. She must; and if you will be so good as to consent, we will withdraw.'

And he led away Gaston with so much authority, that the young man did not even make an attempt at resistance.

When she found that she was alone with the Marquise, Mariette, making an effort to attain composure, rose.

'Madame,' said she, steadying her voice, 'I beg you will be so good as to tell me the meaning of the words you have just uttered, and of the unexpected reception which I have received from you.'

'It is impossible,' said Madame de Saissières, shaking her head.

'And why, madame? There is nothing which it is impossible for me to listen to from your lips.'

'Because I am struggling between the affection I entertain towards you, and the feeling of a duty to be fulfilled towards my grandson.'

'What, madame! Is it possible that these feelings can be in contradiction to one another? What more cruel thing could I possibly hear from you? Explain yourself, madame.'

'I cannot, Mariette. I have not strength just now to speak.'

'I may, perhaps, be able to help you, for I think I understand you. Whatever effort it costs me, I will go forward and meet the blow which you hesitate to inflict upon me. M. le Marquis de Saissières,' continued Mariette, with a mixture of pride and shame, 'has informed you, madame, of the feelings he entertains towards me. You are aware of the avowal he has made me, and—wherefore should I blush to continue?—the fault of which I have been guilty in allowing him to see that I responded to it. I swear before God, madame, that when I fell into this error, I believed that your grandson's sentiments were, as he assured me, approved by you, and approved without reserve. At this moment I am full of doubts and fears. O madame, try and understand, if it be possible, how cruel is the position I occupy in regard to you! Speak, then; explain yourself, if it be only by one single word!'

'My dear, my too dear child,' said the Marquise, taking Mariette's hand in hers, 'I understand but too well the affection Gaston feels towards you. It was necessary to be blind, as I was, it seems, not to comprehend that he could not know you without loving you. Fool that I was, I never saw it. I did nothing to prevent what has happened. I did not even dream that there was any danger. I have been wrong, very wrong.'

'It is enough,' stammered Mariette, closing her eyes. 'I understand.'

Seeing her totter, the aged lady made a superhuman effort to rise from her easy-chair, and not succeeding called for her maids. But Mariette stopped her.

'It is over,' she said, with an effort. 'I beg you will not summon any one.'

And she repeated over and over again, as though speaking to herself,

'It is at an end, it is at an end.'

Then, addressing Madame de Saissières in a calm and gentle voice,

'Might I venture to beg you, Madame la Marquise, to tell me everything? You hesitate to speak because you fear to grieve me. Now that I know the attachment which your son entertains for me is a misfortune in your eyes, do not spare me any longer. I am strong enough to hear whatever you may still have to say to me. I implore you, then, to go on.'

The old lady refused to speak; but at last, by little and little, Mariette learnt that some time before the Marquise had proposed a brilliant alliance to Gaston, and one in which he would have found united together all the advantages of birth, rank, and fortune; an alliance, moreover, which, in the opinion of his grandmother, offered many bright promises for the future, as the young lady was endowed with every amiable and social quality, great external charms, and all the firmness of character which was necessary to secure Gaston's fickle heart.

When the Marquise had finished speaking, Mariette felt herself so humiliated in her own eyes that she could not help inwardly asking, whilst with difficulty restraining her tears, how she could ever have dreamt for a moment, she, a poor and lowly girl, of meriting and retaining Gaston's affection. Involuntarily she allowed to escape from her lips words which rather resembled a sob, so sorrowfully were they whispered,

'And yet he loves me!'

'Alas, my child,' said the Marquise, who had heard what she said, 'how long will it last? He has loved others before you, and they doubtless, like you, flattered themselves that they would be able to preserve his affection.'

Mariette bowed her head in silence. The Marquise still went on speaking for a long time, and at last ended by saying,

'For the rest, my child, do not fear anything from me. I have been scrupulously faithful to the promise which Gaston forced from me. I do not approve your marriage, but I shall know how to keep silence. Whatever may have always been my sentiments with regard to unequal marriages, I will accept the one which my grandson wishes to form, and I will not forget that the brow on which he is about to place the coronet of a Marquise already wears a halo of virtues.'

Marriette did not reply to this peroration. Her uncle and Gaston had come back into the room, and she asked permission to withdraw, to which her uncle eagerly consented. The Marquise shook hands with her, and addressed to her some commonplace affectionate expressions, without being able to rouse her from the stupefaction into which she had fallen. Gaston, who was observing her with sorrowful anxiety, cast upon his grandmother a glance in which respect scarcely softened reproach.

In the evening Mariette had a long conversation with her uncle. She passed the whole night in meditation, in prayer, and in tears. The next day the only strength she possessed came from the fever which was preying upon her. When she saw her uncle enter her room, she went up to him and merely whispered,

'The sacrifice is made.'

And he answered,

'May God bless you and take pity on you, my poor child!'

Gaston came very early in the morning. He was anxious about Mariette's health, and also desired to know on what terms his grandmother had spoken to her. Mariette would have been thankful not to tell him anything, but as soon as he was alone with her he questioned her. She stopped him, however, by a gesture.

'Do not let us talk of your grandmother, who was, as she has ever been, full of kindness towards me. I have something very serious to say to you. Do not look at me in that way. You will agitate me, and I have a sorrowful, a very sorrowful confession to make to you. For a long time past, my dear, I have failed in sincerity towards you; I have hidden my feelings from you. You have been fancying that I was full of the happiness of being loved by you, and of the hope of soon becoming your wife. There has been nothing of the kind. Whilst you were indulging in a happy dream of a future which was to be common to us both, my own mind was ill at ease, my heart was troubled. I was afraid of being deceived as to the nature of my sentiments. What shall I say to you, Gaston? I felt as though, in order to exchange the peaceful and quiet life, which had become a necessity, for the brilliant lot which you destined for me, and also in order to accept the little bitternesses of an unequal alliance, it was requisite to—forgive me for saying so to you, Gaston—to love you more than I can, above all in a different way from that in which I do.'

'Mariette,' exclaimed Gaston, in a tone of anguish, 'in the name of Heaven, what is it you are saying? I am losing my reason! It cannot be you who are addressing me thus, Mariette!'

'Yes, my dear, it is I; it is really I, alas, who am making this humiliating confession. I have deferred it only too long. I could not help it; I had no courage.'

Gaston had risen. He looked at her without being able to utter a word. Turning her eyes away, she continued,

'You will reproach me, perhaps, for having inflicted a bitter disappointment upon you. If it be so, I can only entreat you to forgive me. Yesterday I suddenly felt as though I were able to explain myself to your grandmother. I was going to ask her to speak to you in my name, and conjure you to renounce me. But I thought that, perhaps, it would be less sad for you to receive such an entreaty from my own lips; and although it would, I knew, cost me much more to speak to you myself, I felt that I ought.'

'Mariette,' cried Gaston, in a broken voice, 'I do not understand the meaning of your words! No; it is not possible! In the name of Heaven, explain yourself! Do you mean to say—I cannot utter the words! Do you mean to tell me that you do not love me?'

'Yes and no, Gaston. I love you, but it is with an affection entirely different from that which would be necessary, in order that I should become your wife. At first, agitated by the ardent expressions to which you gave utterance of the feelings with which I had inspired you, I deceived myself, I confess, as to those which I myself entertained. But after-reflection has enlightened me. Gaston, give me up. You must; I cannot render you happy.'

'I am the sole judge of *that*,' exclaimed the Marquis impetuously.

'No,' said Mariette; 'and I will show you in one word that it is my feelings alone which ought to decide our fate. If I tell you, my dear, that I cannot make you happy, it is because I know that I myself should be unhappy.'

The young man's despair burst forth in cries, in complaints, in reproaches. Mariette listened to him with her head bent, only whispering,

'Forgive me, forgive me!'

'It is my grandmother,' exclaimed Gaston impetuously and in a rage,—'it is my grandmother who has dictated this language to you!'

'Do not accuse your grandmother,' said Mariette earnestly. 'She has been scrupulously faithful to the promise she made you, and she anew confirmed her full assent to our marriage.'

'It is, then, spontaneously, and with your own free

will, that you speak to me in this way!' cried Gaston.

'Spontaneously, and with my own free will.'

'Swear it! I will believe your oath.'

'I swear it.'

Gaston uttered a stifled cry, and rushed out of the room.

At the same moment the Curé entered. He found Mariette on her knees, her face bathed in tears.

'He will forget me,' she murmured.

The Curé sat down beside her, and laid her head on his knees. All at once she looked up, stifled her sobs, and fixing on her uncle an eager gaze, she exclaimed,

'But if he should not forget me?'

'Then, as now, my child, you will be free. But for the sake of his happiness and of your repose, God grant that he may forget you!'

'You are right,' she said; 'for then I alone shall suffer.'

When Gaston went to the presbytery the following day, Johanna told him that the Curé and his niece had gone away early in the morning; and she then handed him a letter from Mariette.

'Forgive me, dear friend,' she said. 'To see you again just now would be more than I could bear. I feel that I have been too guilty towards you, and the sight of your sorrow is a reproach which overwhelms me with grief. Besides, I could only repeat what I said to you yesterday. I do not look upon love in the same light that you do, and I do not find in my heart that which is requisite in order that our marriage may be a happy one. I entreat you to make an effort for my sake. That effort is, to forget me. The feelings with which I have inspired you cannot, in so short a time, have taken very deep root in your heart. Farewell! Be happy. If you should still think of me, let it be without anger. I am going to retire for some little time into the convent, of which our good Johanna's cousin is the superior. There I shall meet with every kindness, care, and attention. Do not make any attempt to see me again. The sight of you would be painful to me. I tell you so plainly. Embrace your grandmother for me, and beg her to bless me.'

'Ungrateful girl!' exclaimed Gaston, crushing the letter in his clenched hands.'

And the following day he left the château with his soul full of despair, but quite resolved to tear from his heart—alas, but too prompt to forget!—a hopeless love.

CHAPTER XVIII.

A MONTH afterwards Mariette, who had returned in an almost dying state to the presbytery, was stretched upon her bed. On one side of it her uncle was kneeling, on the other side Gaston de Saissières, who, summoned in haste, had come to assist at the last moments of the young girl, who was dying for him. They each of them held one of poor Mariette's hands, and were watching on her face the progress of death, which was drawing near. A noise at the door of the room caused them to direct their eyes towards it. It was the Marquise de Saissières, who, without having mentioned it to any one, had had herself conveyed to the presbytery. By means of almost miraculous efforts, and supported by one of her women, she succeeded in placing herself on her knees beside the bed. Mariette, who had seen her, exhibited signs of agitation.

'Marie du Reux,' then said the aged lady, in a hollow voice, 'may your forgiveness and your blessing descend upon the head of the Marquise de Saissières!'

The dying girl, suddenly recalled, as it were, to life, said a few words to her uncle, who helped her to lay her hand upon the white locks of the Marquise. Mariette tried to speak; but the words expired on her lips, and, no longer having strength even to turn her head on her pillow, she cast a glance of tenderness on her uncle and on Gaston alternately. Then the priest, with a gesture of resignation, gently took hold of the beloved head, and, turning the face of his niece towards the young man, 'Look at her!' he whispered.

And if he had been able to see the last ray of happiness and of love which shone in Mariette's eyes, he would have been repaid for this supreme sacrifice. It was Gaston who alone beheld that gaze, so sweet, so pure, so tender, veil itself, little by little, and then become for ever extinguished, whilst Mariette's last sigh was noiselessly exhaled from between her half-opened lips.

* * * *

Two days later, the young girls of the village bore to the cemetery a little coffin, whose sombre form was hardly discernible beneath the white pall reserved for young maidens.

On the edge of the grave, M. le Curé stood upright, like an old oak struck by lightning. It was he who cast the first handful of earth upon the coffin as it was lowered into its tomb. At the moment when the earth which had been cast upon it gave forth a hollow sound, a piercing terrible cry, which suddenly resounded through the air, made the bystanders shudder. It was the Curé who had uttered it. The spade fell out of his trembling hand, he stretched forth his arms, and tottered. Those who were standing near the grave hastened towards him; but gently putting aside the persons who were trying to support him, he said aloud, 'May the will of God be done, my children, and may it be for ever blessed!'

And the sorrowful ceremony was at an end.

The poor priest lived for several years afterwards, without anything beyond a smile ever lighting up his austere melancholy face. Then God took pity on him, and permitted him to die. Some time before, Johanna had already rejoined her young mistress.

The Marquise de Saissières survived Mariette a few days only.

The Marquis, whose feelings had been strongly re-awakened on beholding once more her whom he had loved, believed himself to be inconsolable, until a time came when he found consolation. He remained ignorant to the last of the sacrifice Mariette had made for his sake.

Finally there remained no one in the village, excepting big Joseph, who, now that he was old, and, as always, averse to work, lived upon charity.

Sometimes he went to the cemetery to look at a little tombstone, on which was inscribed only one word, 'Mariette.'

LONDON:
ROBSON AND SONS, PRINTERS, PANCRAS ROAD, N.W.

www.ingramcontent.com/pod-product-compliance
Lightning Source LLC
Chambersburg PA
CBHW032141230426
43672CB00011B/2409